Limited Company Formation

Made Easy™

Limited Company Formation Made Easy

1st edition 1999
   Reprinted 2002
2nd edition 2005

© 2005 Lawpack Publishing Limited

Lawpack Publishing Limited
76–89 Alscot Road
London SE1 3AW

www.lawpack.co.uk

ISBN 1 904053 98 X

Exclusion of Liability and Disclaimer

Contents

Introduction   v

1 Should you incorporate?   1
What is a private limited company?   1
Should you incorporate your business?   2
Types of company   6

2 Creating and naming a private limited company   9
Creating a private limited company   9
Naming your company   11
Use of the company name   12
The registered office   13

3 Filling out the forms   15
How to form your company   15
Memorandum of Association   16
Form 10   16
Articles of Association   17
Form 12   18

4 After incorporation   21
Issuing shares   22
Share certificates   22
Opening a bank account   23
Auditors   23
The transfer of assets to the corporation   25
Taxation   25
Statutory books   26
Company seal   27
Annual return   27
Annual accounts   28
Elective resolutions   29

5 Management of the company 31

Company directors 31

Company secretary 33

6 The shareholders 35

Capital of the company 35

Transfer of shares 37

Shareholders' meetings 37

Written resolutions 41

7 Post-incorporation changes 43

Appointment or removal of the company secretary 43

Appointment or removal of auditors 44

Location of the registered office 44

The name of the company 45

Increase in company capital 45

Allotting shares 45

The objects clause 45

The Articles of Association 46

The accounting reference date 46

Glossary 47

List of sensitive words 51

Appendix: Example forms 59

Index 117

This Lawpack book is 'web enabled', meaning it is supported online with extra material. To access this, all you have to do is to register on the Lawpack website entering the code below.

Registration code: **B7033240905**

Introduction

This *Made Easy* Guide contains the information, instruction and examples of forms necessary to set up your own limited liability company. It is for people forming a company in England, Wales or Scotland. It is not suitable for Northern Ireland, nor for subsidiaries of overseas companies.

This Guide can help you achieve a business and legal objective conveniently, efficiently and economically. Nevertheless, it is important to use this Guide properly if you are to avoid later difficulties. Follow these guidelines:

1. This Guide contains all the basic instructions you need to complete forms which are reproduced in this Guide. If, after thorough examination, you decide that your requirements are not met by this Guide, or you do not feel confident about completing your own documents, then consult a solicitor.

2. We have provided you with examples of the Companies House forms you will need to obtain and complete to set up your company. To help you run your company after incorporation, we have provided example formats of standard minutes, and completed examples of registers. All of these forms can be downloaded from our website.

3. Always use pen or type on legal documents; never use pencil.

4. Do not cross out or erase anything you have written on your final forms.

5. You will find a helpful glossary of terms in this Guide. Refer to this glossary if you find unfamiliar terms.

6. Always keep legal documents in a safe place. Registers, minutes, Memorandum and Articles of Association and the original Certificate of Incorporation should be kept at the company's registered office.

7. If you have any queries about what information should be filed with the Registrar of Companies, contact Companies House, Crown Way, Maindy, Cardiff CF14 3UZ for companies registered in England and Wales. For information on Scottish companies, contact Companies House, 37 Castle Terrace, Edinburgh EH1 2EB. Companies House products and services are also detailed on its website at www.companieshouse.gov.uk or you can call its Contact Centre for information on 0870 333 3636.

CHAPTER 1

Should you incorporate?

What you'll find in this chapter

✔ What is a private limited company?
✔ Should you incorporate your business?
✔ Types of company

This *Made Easy* Guide is intended for the entrepreneur who wants to incorporate a business. The demands of running or starting a business often prevent owners from carefully considering their options, assessing their situations and doing the necessary planning to organise their business to the best advantage.

In this Guide, the private limited company is compared and contrasted to two other business entities: the sole trader and the partnership. The structure, advantages and disadvantages of each are explained below. Completed examples of forms for incorporating your business are included, as well as step-by-step instructions for filling them in. In addition, valuable post-incorporation information about managing and changing your company's structure is included.

What is a private limited company?

A private limited company is:

• a legal entity in its own right distinct from its members;

- owned by its members;
- run by directors, who are appointed by the members;
- empowered to do anything contained in the objects clause of its charter, known as the Memorandum of Association.

If the company is limited by shares, your financial responsibility as a shareholder is limited to paying for your shares in full. This means that provided you have paid for your shares in full, your personal assets cannot be touched, even if the company cannot pay its debts.

 If a shareholder subscribes £1,000 for one thousand £1 shares and the company becomes insolvent, owing millions of pounds in debt, the most he can lose is £1,000.

Should you incorporate your business?

Whether you are currently running a business or planning to start a new enterprise, you should consider carefully the various types of business organisation that exist.

The three basic types of business entity are: sole trader, partnership and limited company. Each offers its own advantages and disadvantages.

Sole traders

Operating as a sole trader is the simplest form of business.

As a sole trader you are in charge of all aspects of the business. You are personally liable for all debts of the business, even in excess of the amount invested. You and the business are considered the same entity.

The advantages of being a sole trader are:

1. No requirement to file accounts or annual returns or other information at Companies House, which means you have greater privacy.

2. You are in complete control of the business.

3. Possible tax advantages.

The disadvantages are:

1. Unlimited liability. You will be responsible for any amount of business debts no matter how incurred, which means that your personal property can be used to settle business debts. This, of course, is a significant disadvantage.

2. Difficulty in raising capital because you cannot transfer an interest in the business to investors as security for their investment.

 As a sole trader, your personal property can be used to settle business debts; this is a significant disadvantage!

Partnerships

A partnership involves two or more individuals carrying on a business together with a view to profit. Each partner is personally liable for all debts of the partnership, including those incurred by the other partners. Partnership agreements can be quite complex.

The advantages of a partnership are:

1. Broader management base than a sole trader.

2. Possible tax advantages, by avoiding double taxation whereby the company pays Corporation Tax on its profit and the shareholders pay Capital Gains Tax on the sale of their shares or Income Tax on dividends.

The disadvantages of a partnership are:

1. Unlimited liability of all the partners. The personal assets of each partner are available to satisfy debts of the partnership.

2. The partnership may come to an end when existing partners leave or die. If there are two partners and one leaves or dies, the remaining partner becomes a sole trader.

3. Obtaining large sums of capital is relatively difficult as investment cannot be obtained from new shareholders.

4. Business decisions taken by just one partner bind all the partners.

5. It may not be easy to sell or transfer an individual partnership interest.

6. Some tax incentives, such as employee share option schemes, are not available to partnerships.

Since April 2001, new 'limited liability partnerships' have also existed; details are available from Companies House. Tax legislation may determine how popular this business structure proves.

 If you want to set up a partnership, you can use Lawpack's *Business Partnership Agreement (F211)*, available from stationers and bookshops as well as our website at www.lawpack.co.uk.

Companies

There are several distinct advantages to forming a company, which can be done individually or in concert with one or more investors or shareholders. Of course, the benefits of having limited liability and easily raising capital may not outweigh the disadvantages of higher costs, increased paperwork and greater regulation to which you will be subjected once you form a company.

The advantages of a company are:

1. Limited liability. The shareholders are not personally liable for the debts of the company. The company can only ask shareholders to pay for their shares in full. The shareholder's responsibility is limited to this amount and this amount is determined when the shareholder agrees to buy shares. Should the business fail, the creditors cannot obtain possession of shareholders' assets, such as homes or cars, in settlement of debts. Limited liability is the most important reason why so many businesses are incorporated.

2.   Capital can be raised with relative ease because investors can buy shares in the company. This does not mean, however, that a new company can simply offer shares to the public. Share offers are regulated by law.

3.   Subject to the Articles of Association, shares can be transferred to existing members and to family members as gifts or otherwise. It is possible to sell your shares to other people, but not in a general offer to the public. Investors in a private company do not receive the same protection as they would have if they were investing in companies listed on the Stock Exchange.

4.   Since the company is an independent legal entity, it does not cease to exist because one of the shareholders dies or retires. It is therefore easier to ensure continuity with a company than with a partnership.

The disadvantages of a company are:

1.   It must comply with statutory rules and disclose information to the public.

2.   It is usually the most expensive form of business to organise and run, although a partnership can be equally expensive.

3.   Both the company and the individual shareholder have to make tax returns.

4.   Record keeping (such as keeping a minute book) can be more extensive for a company.

5.   Winding up a company and in many cases even changing its structure can be more complicated and expensive than for partnerships and sole traders.

The choice of the structure for your business should be considered carefully. Once you have decided that a company is the appropriate structure for your business, you must go through the legal steps required to create your company. With careful planning most people can easily set up and run their own company without needing a solicitor, thus saving substantial legal fees.

The benefits of having limited liability and raising capital may not outweigh the disadvantages of higher costs, increased paperwork and greater regulation to which you will be subjected once you form a limited company.

Types of company

The liability of the shareholder is determined by the type of company formed:

Limited by shares

The shareholder's liability is limited to the nominal value of the shares held by the shareholder. If the shareholder has agreed to pay more than the nominal value, the liability is for that greater sum. Provided the company is successful, the value of the shares should increase, but if the company goes into liquidation, the shareholder can lose this investment.

Limited by guarantee

The member's liability is limited to an amount the member has personally guaranteed to contribute to the assets of the company if it is wound up; this guarantee also applies for a period of one year after membership has ceased. This type of company has no share capital.

Unlimited company

The shareholder's liability is not limited and the shareholder could be asked to pay the company's debts.

Public limited company

The shareholder's liability will be limited to the nominal value of the shares held by the shareholder. If the shareholder has agreed to pay more than the nominal value, the liability is for that greater sum. On incorporation, the company's name and Memorandum of Association must specify that it is a public limited company. The statutory rules which a public company must comply with are stricter than those which apply to private companies.

CHAPTER 2

Creating and naming a private limited company

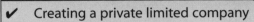

What you'll find in this chapter

- ✔ Creating a private limited company
- ✔ Naming your company
- ✔ Use of the company name
- ✔ The registered office

Creating a private limited company

By following the instructions in this *Made Easy* Guide and downloading and completing the forms provided on Lawpack's website (see page 59), you will be able to set up a private limited company along the following lines:

- It can operate with a minimum of one director or with two or more directors who is/are responsible for the management of the company.

- A company secretary, who can be one of the two directors. The secretary is responsible for the administration of the company and compliance with filing requirements. If the company only has one director, a different person must act as company secretary.

- Authorised share capital of £100, made up of 100 shares, each with a nominal value of £1. It is possible to issue shares at a higher value so that the company has more capital (see chapter 6, 'The shareholders').

- A registered office in England or Wales, so that English law applies, or in Scotland, so that Scots law applies.

 All aspects of the company can be changed later, although certain formalities (and possibly fees) will be required. If you make any changes to the constitutional arrangements, you must notify Companies House.

The documents needed for incorporation, examples of which are included in this *Made Easy* Guide, are as follows:

1. **Memorandum of Association** sets out the name of the company, where the registered office is situated, the objects for which the company was set up, the liability of the members and the authorised share capital.

2. **Form 10** gives details of the directors, company secretary and the address of the registered office.

3. **Articles of Association** contain the company's regulations for its internal management.

4. **Form 12** states that the directors have complied with all proper procedures to form a company.

A fifth requirement is the fee for incorporation. Companies House can advise on the current amount (tel 0870 333 3636).

It should be noted that currently approximately 80 per cent of companies are incorporated electronically. Companies House imposes quite stringent software requirements on 'presenters' and company formation agents can offer access to their formation software packages through their websites. Prices for formations can range from £50 upwards. The insertion of certain items of security information dispenses with the need for signatures and there is also no need to have the Form 12 signed (see below). Currently, the Companies House formation fee for a company incorporated by electronic means is £5 less than a paper-based incorporation.

Naming your company

Once you are ready to set up your company, you must choose a company name and then determine whether you are allowed to use that name. The following points should be noted:

1. **The name must include the word 'Limited' at the end of it.** If you are incorporating a company in Wales (i.e. its registered office is in Wales), the name may be written in either English or Welsh. The Welsh word for 'Limited' is 'Cyfyngedig'. You can also use the abbreviations 'Ltd' or 'Cyf'.

2. You cannot use a name for your company which:

    a) Is identical to a name already on the Register at Companies House.

    b) Is so similar as to be considered the same as or too like a name on the Register. For example:

    (i) Lawpack Publishing Limited

    Lawpack Publishing Company Limited

    The above names would be considered the same.

    (ii) Lawpack Publishing Limited

    Law Pak Publishing Limited

    The above names would not be refused initially, as they are not identical; the lower company may have to change its name on a successful objection from the upper company.

    c) Is offensive or would constitute a criminal offence.

    d) Is so misleading as to the activities of the company that it causes harm to the public.

    e) Gives the impression that the company is connected with HM Government or a local authority.

    f) Includes any sensitive words or expressions listed on pages 51–55.

If you have any doubts about your choice of name, consult Companies House.

When a name is accepted for registration, it does not mean it can be used as a trade mark. Trade mark searches are separate and must be done at the Trade Marks Registry.

Use of the company name

As soon as your company is incorporated you are required to publish its name on business stationery and at the business premises.

Place of business

You must paint or affix your company name outside any office or place of business of your company. The name should be conspicuous and easily legible.

Business stationery

Your company name should appear on:

- all company business letters;
- all notices and other official publications;
- all bills of exchange, promissory notes, endorsements, cheques, and orders for money or goods by or on behalf of the company;
- all bills of parcels, invoices, receipts and letters of credit.

You must use your company name exactly as it appears on your Certificate of Incorporation. Remember to include the word 'Limited' or 'Ltd'.

If your company is registered in Wales and the company name includes the word 'Cyfyngedig' or 'Cyf', you must also state in English that the company is Limited on all business stationery and in the name displayed at the business premises.

You are required to specify the following additional information on your business letters and company order forms:

- place of registration (i.e. registered in England and Wales, Wales or Scotland);
- registration number (on your Certificate of Incorporation);
- registered office address (see below).

Trade names

If your company trades under a different name from its registered name, you may be personally liable for its debts, unless you state the company's registered name on its business stationery.

The registered office

Often this will be your company's office. You could alternatively use the address of your solicitor or accountant, but he may make a charge for this.

This *Made Easy* Guide is only suitable for forming a company with a registered office in England, Wales or Scotland.

 If a company trades under a different name from its registered name, the directors may be personally liable for its debts. To avoid this, be sure to state your company's registered name on all business stationery.

CHAPTER 3

Filling out the forms

What you'll find in this chapter

✔ How to form your company
✔ Memorandum of Association
✔ Form 10
✔ Articles of Association
✔ Form 12

How to form your company

In order to form your limited company, the following four documents must be completed and then filed together at Companies House:

1. **Memorandum of Association** (see page 61)

2. **Form 10: First directors and secretary and intended situation of registered office** (see page 96)

3. **Articles of Association** (see page 63)

4. **Form 12: Declaration on application for registration** (see page 100)

You must be consistent with wording when referring to your company name on all documents filed at Companies House. Choose 'Limited' or 'Ltd', or 'Cyfyngedig' or 'Cyf', but do not use both.

Memorandum of Association

This is the company's charter, which lists all of the activities the company is entitled to do. A company which pursues activities outside its stated scope can run into problems, and so the Memorandum provided in this *Made Easy* Guide has been broadly drafted to give your company the right to conduct any trade or business whatsoever.

In addition, the Memorandum provides for:

- Authorised capital of £100 divided into 100 shares of £1 each.
- Two subscribers (who become the first shareholders of the company); alternatively, an option is available for a one-member private limited company.
- One share of £1 each, held by the sole subscriber or both subscribers.

What you must do:

- Fill in the company's name in the two spaces provided.
- Delete either 'England and Wales' or 'Scotland' according to where your company's registered office is to be.
- State the number of shares to be taken by each subscriber and the total number.
- The subscriber or the two subscribers should state his/their name and address.
- The subscriber or the two subscribers should sign his/their respective name in the presence of a witness, who should sign the Memorandum as such and state his name and address.
- The Memorandum should be dated on the day it is signed.

Form 10

This is the statement of the first directors and secretary and the intended location of the registered office. You must provide the following:

- the company name;
- the address of the registered office;
- personal details of the company secretary, including:
    - full name;
    - residential address.

The secretary must sign and date Form 10.

- personal details of the directors, including:
    - full name;
    - residential address;
    - date of birth;
    - business occupation;
    - nationality;
    - other UK directorships;
- an address for correspondence (see page 1 of Form 10).

Each director must sign and date Form 10.

At the bottom of page 3 of Form 10 there are several signature boxes. Unless an agent is acting on your behalf the one or two subscribers who signed the Memorandum must each sign and date the relevant boxes.

Articles of Association

The Articles of Association are the rules by which the company must be run by the directors and shareholders. A standard set of Articles of Association which a private company limited by shares may adopt is provided by Table A of the Companies Act 1985. This *Made Easy* Guide makes provision for the setting up of a company in England, Wales or Scotland with this standard set of Articles of Association, with some modifications. The most important of these is found in Article 26, which provides that where a person wants to transfer his shares in the company he must first offer to sell them to existing shareholders. In addition, it gives the directors power to refuse to register any share transfer.

You should read the Articles of Association included in this *Made Easy* Guide to check that they are suitable for your needs. Note in particular the provisions concerning quorums at general meetings (Article 42) and meetings of the directors (Article 88), and directors' interests in resolutions of the company (Article 93).

If you do not understand any of the provisions in the Articles of Association or any provision seems inappropriate for your company, you should consult a solicitor. If you are satisfied with the Articles of Association included in this *Made Easy* Guide, then you should carry out the following steps:

1. Fill in the company's name in the space provided at the top of the first page of the Articles.

2. The subscriber or the two subscribers to the Memorandum should state their name and address at the end of the Articles.

3. The subscriber or the two subscribers must sign and date the Articles in the presence of a witness, who should also sign as evidence of such and state his name and address.

4. The Articles should be dated on the day of signing.

Form 12

One of the directors or the secretary (either of whom has signed Form 10) makes an official declaration that all the requirements for registration of the company have been met.

The declaration is self-explanatory and must be made and signed in the presence of a notary public, commissioner for oaths (who can be a solicitor with a practising certificate) or a justice of the peace. A nominal fee is charged for this.

After completing your forms and documents, send the Memorandum, Articles of Association, Forms 10 and 12, together with a cheque for the fee payable, to:

for England and Wales: or   **for Scotland:**

Registrar of Companies   Registrar of Companies
Companies House   Companies House
Crown Way   37 Castle Terrace
Maindy   Edinburgh EH1 2EB
Cardiff CF14 3UZ

Take copies before sending off the originals, as Companies House charges for issuing copies of submitted documents.

The Registrar will then send you a Certificate of Incorporation. The company comes into existence from the date stated on the Certificate of Incorporation.

CHAPTER 4
After incorporation

What you'll find in this chapter

✔ Issuing shares
✔ Share certificates
✔ Opening a bank account
✔ Auditors
✔ The transfer of assets to the corporation
✔ Taxation
✔ Statutory books
✔ Company seal
✔ Annual return
✔ Annual accounts
✔ Elective resolutions

Once your company is incorporated there are certain legal requirements to be fulfilled. There are also various practical considerations to be dealt with, some of which will be appropriate to you.

To achieve these objectives, you will need to hold a meeting of all the directors, which is called a Board meeting, to discuss and agree upon the items listed below. The decisions of all Board meetings must be recorded in writing, in what are known as the Board minutes. An example format of Board minutes is provided for you on page 105. Alternatively, all the directors can sign a written resolution (see page 107).

The following should be dealt with whether a Board meeting is called or a written resolution used:

1. issuing shares;

2. share certificates;

3. opening a bank account;

4. appointment of auditors.

Some practical considerations which could also be discussed at your first Board meeting are:

5. the transfer of assets;

6. tax issues.

Issuing shares

The directors should allot and issue one share of £1 each to each of the subscribers to the Memorandum. A majority of the directors must agree to do so at the Board meeting.

There is no need to notify the allotment of the subscriber shares to Companies House; the subscription to the Memorandum of Association is sufficient. Companies House must be notified within one month of the allotment of any further shares. Notification is given by completing and filing Form G88(2), an example of which is included on page 101. You should complete yours according to your own requirements. A Register of Members (see below) should be completed by the secretary to show the one or two subscribers as members of the company. If the company is a single-member company, the Companies Act 1985 requires that a statement to this effect be made in the Register of Members. This statement normally reads as follows: 'In accordance with section 352A of the Companies Act 1985 the company has become a one-member private limited company with effect from [*insert date*] with the sole member being [*insert name and address of member*].'

Share certificates

To provide the shareholders with a title document to their shares, you will need to issue share certificates at the first Board meeting. Each must include the following:

- a certificate number;
- the number of shares;
- the name of the company;
- the name of the holder;
- the address of the holder;
- the number and type of shares issued to the holder;
- the nominal value of the shares;
- a statement of the extent to which the shares are paid up.

If you have a company seal (see page 27), this can be stamped on the certificate in the presence of either two directors, or one director and the company secretary. If you do not have a seal, the certificate can merely be signed as above. The certificate should be dated on issue.

Opening a bank account

To open a company bank account, the directors must pass a resolution of approval.

Auditors

The company is, subject to the exceptions mentioned below, obliged by law to file annual audited accounts (i.e. approved by a registered auditor). The directors must pass a resolution appointing auditors for the company; the auditors must be independent, i.e. not employees of the company.

Your company will need to prepare accounts for each financial year. Your first financial year may be shorter or longer than a year and will begin on the date of incorporation and end on the last day of its 'accounting reference' period.

Unless you change it, your accounting reference date will automatically fall on the last day of the month in which the anniversary of the company's incorporation falls. To change the accounting reference date, you can give notice to the Registrar of Companies using Form 225. Thereafter, a company can change its accounting reference date either during its current accounting period, or during the period allowed for delivering the accounts in question. A company cannot extend an accounting period more than once in five years unless certain circumstances apply. You should fill in the following:

- company number;
- name of company;
- day, month and year of the company's shortened or extended accounting reference period.

In addition:

- the form must be signed by either a director or the company secretary and you should indicate which by deleting accordingly;
- date the form and give the company's name and address in the box provided to enable Companies House to correspond with you.

With certain exceptions, a company may qualify for exemption from the requirements of having an audit if it qualifies as a 'small company'. In summary, a 'small company' must have two of the following three characteristics:

1. a turnover not exceeding £5.6 million;
2. a balance sheet not exceeding £2.8 million;
3. an average number of employees not exceeding 50.

In any case, members holding not less than ten per cent in nominal value of any class of shares may, by written notice no later than one month before the end of a financial year, require the company to obtain an audit for that year.

If your company is a 'small company' and has not entered into any transactions of accounting significance in the period under review, it may qualify as a 'dormant company' and avoid the need to appoint auditors or have an auditor's report with the accounts.

Your accountant will be able to advise you on taking advantage of any of the above exemptions.

The transfer of assets to the corporation

If you have been operating a business prior to incorporation, you can transfer the assets and debts of the business to the new company at an agreed sum and receive shares in exchange. You cannot, however, burden your company with more debt than assets. You cannot sell your personal property to the company at inflated prices or exchange company shares for personal property that is overvalued. If a director wishes to buy a non-cash asset from the company or dispose of such an asset to the company, and that asset is above a certain statutory value, the shareholders must approve the transaction in a general meeting, or by written resolution. Your accountant can advise you on this. You will also need to consult your solicitor on how to effect the transfer of your assets to the company.

The directors will also need to pass an appropriate resolution which must be documented in the Board minutes. Stamp duty may be payable on documents relating to the transfer of assets (e.g. property).

Taxation

You will need to contact your local tax office if you are employing staff, including paid directors, who are employees of the company. The tax office will provide you with the documents required to operate a PAYE (pay as you earn) scheme and tell you how to make National Insurance contributions.

You should contact HM Revenue & Customs to find out whether you need to register for VAT (Value Added Tax):

for England and Wales:	**or**	**for Scotland:**
HM Revenue & Customs		HM Revenue & Customs
King's Beam House		Caledonian House
39–41 Mark Lane		Greenmarket
London EC3R 7HE		Dundee DD1 1HD
Tel 020 7626 1515		Tel 01382 200 822

Your accountant will be able to help you with queries concerning Corporation Tax and Capital Gains Tax.

Statutory books

You must maintain certain records about the company's meetings, directors and shareholders, known as statutory books. These are kept for the benefit of the shareholders and the general public.

In this *Made Easy* Guide you will find completed examples of some of these registers (templates of all of the registers are available to download from our website):

1. **Register of Members.**

2. **Register of Directors.**

3. **Register of Secretaries.**

4. **Register of Directors' Interests.** This records the directors' interests in shares or debentures of the company and its associated companies together with any interest of a spouse or child.

5. **Register of Charges.** This records charges (i.e. financial liabilities or commitments) over the property of the company.

Each of the registers should be kept at the company's registered office or, in certain circumstances, at another address within the country of incorporation; Companies House does require to be notified if registers are kept outside the registered office. You should complete all the information requested on the sample forms. Shareholders can inspect the statutory books free of charge, but the company may charge anyone else a nominal fee.

The company must also maintain accounting records. Your accountant will be able to advise you on the accounting records which need to be kept. In addition, copies of the directors' service contracts, if any, and copies of any charges (loans secured on the company's assets) must be kept by the company and be available for inspection to any member of the company.

Minute book

A minute book is a record of Board and shareholder meetings and can take the form of a file. You are legally required to keep a minute book. Board meetings (see page 105) and shareholder meetings must be fully recorded in writing. Written resolutions (see page 107) must also be noted in a minute book. Minutes must be signed by a director or chairperson and filed in the minute book.

Remember that the company must maintain a continuous and up-to-date record of all its actions approved by shareholders and/or directors.

Company seal

There is no longer a legal obligation to have a company seal. If you decide to have a company seal, it can be ordered from a legal stationer. The seal is stamped on a document and witnessed by a director and the secretary or by two directors of the company. Remember, use of the seal should be authorised by the Board (see Article 97). Whether or not the company has a seal, a document which is signed by a director and the secretary or by two directors of the company 'on behalf of XYZ Company Limited' has the same effect as if executed under the seal of the company.

Annual return

Your company must deliver an annual return to Companies House relating to all business carried out up to the anniversary of the company's incorporation. It must be in the form prescribed by Companies House, known as a Form 363, signed by a director or secretary of the company and sent with a cheque for the fee payable. Companies House will automatically send a Form 363 to you.

If the company fails to deliver its annual return within 28 days after the return date, the company is liable to a fine, as is every director and the company secretary.

Companies House offers an online facility for submitting annual returns. A recent price change means that an annual return filed online can be £15 cheaper than a paper-based annual return. Contact Companies House for details of the web filing service.

If the company's annual return is more than 28 days late, the company is liable to a fine, as is every director and the company secretary.

Annual accounts

The company must prepare and file at Companies House annual company accounts consisting of a balance sheet and a profit and loss account made up to the last day of the company's financial year. The company must file a directors' report and, if appropriate, an auditor's report with each set of annual accounts. The accounts must be delivered to Companies House within ten months after the end of the relevant accounting reference period. If the company fails to file such accounts, it is liable to a fine, as is each director. Certain exemptions as to the information that needs to be filed are available; your accountant should be able to advise you on this.

The accounts and directors' report must be approved by the directors and signed on behalf of the Board by a director or, in the case of the directors' report, by the secretary or a director. The auditor's report must be signed by the auditors.

If a company trades in Wales, the accounts may be in Welsh, but a certified English translation must be attached when they are submitted to Companies House.

Generally, the accounts and directors' and auditor's reports are laid, or presented, before the company's shareholders at a general meeting. By passing an elective resolution (see below) a company can dispense with this requirement.

Elective resolutions

Annual General Meetings of shareholders (AGMs) must be held to lay the annual accounts and directors' and auditor's reports before the shareholders, and to deal with other matters such as the annual appointment of auditors. However, private companies can pass elective resolutions dispensing with the laying of accounts and reports before the shareholders, with the annual appointment of auditors and with Annual General Meetings. In this *Made Easy* Guide we have included an example format of elective resolutions (see page 115) which allow the company to dispense with these requirements. These are for reference when preparing your own.

Where the company has passed an elective resolution dispensing with the laying of accounts and reports before the shareholders, the shareholders must be provided with the company's annual accounts together with the directors' report and the auditor's report. They are entitled to receive the above documents at least 28 days before the accounts are due to be delivered to Companies House. Shareholders must be informed of their right to require the laying of accounts and reports before the general meeting and any shareholder can enforce this right.

 Remember, the company must notify Companies House of changes to the company's constitution, share capital and management. You should consult Companies House if you have queries concerning the information to be filed.

CHAPTER 5

Management of the company

The following background information will help you understand how to run your company.

Company directors

The directors' responsibility is to run the company on behalf of the shareholders. Directors have extensive powers delegated by the shareholders in the Articles of Association (see Article 72). But shareholders can dismiss directors by following specific procedures and passing an ordinary resolution at a meeting of shareholders. Shareholders holding a simple majority (either alone or collectively with other shareholders) of the issued shares of the company will be able to remove a director and control the Board. This is provided that at least 28 days before the meeting a member has given notice to the company of his intention to propose the resolution (this is known as a special notice), and the company has in turn given the members notice of the resolution 21 days before the meeting. Where special notice has been given, there are no provisions in the Companies Act 1985 to enable the general meeting to be held on short notice. If a director is to be removed from office, the company, the director and the member(s) proposing the removal should seek legal advice.

Directors are obliged to act in good faith and in the best interests of the company. They must avoid placing themselves in a position where there is or might be a conflict between their personal interest and their duty to the company. They must exercise skill and care in their role as directors.

Sometimes the directors and shareholders are the same people although there is no requirement that they should be.

Directors' proceedings

Generally, the management of the company will be carried out by the directors. Decisions will be taken at Board meetings.

1. The Articles specify that two directors must be present at Board meetings (unless there is only one director, when that person will form a quorum).

2. All the directors in the UK must receive reasonable notice of a Board meeting (see Article 87). Resolutions are passed by a majority of the directors at the Board meeting. The example company in this *Made Easy* Guide has the option of operating with one or two, or more, directors and does not provide the chairperson with a casting vote (i.e. a second vote in addition to his director's vote). Should your company grow and the number of directors increase, you may want to amend your Articles to include a chairperson's casting vote to avoid a possible impasse at Board meetings.

3. A record of Board meetings must be kept. The record is known as Board minutes.

4. If the directors do not wish to hold a Board meeting, they can pass a written resolution provided that all the directors sign that resolution (see Article 92). The resolution is dated when the last director signs it and it is entered in the minute book.

In practice the day-to-day running of the company will be delegated by the Board of directors to one or more of them so that it is unnecessary to hold Board meetings on many matters. However, certain activities will require the directors to act collectively in a meeting (e.g. allotment of shares to shareholders).

 Sometimes the directors and shareholders are the same people, although there is no requirement that they should be.

Appointment of directors

The first directors are named in the incorporation documents (Form 10), filed with Companies House. They are deemed appointed on incorporation (i.e. date on Certificate of Incorporation). Additional directors may be appointed by either the Board of directors or the shareholders (see Articles 76 to 79).

Other considerations

There are many issues concerning company directors which cannot be covered in this *Made Easy* Guide (e.g. loans made to directors, substantial property transactions between the director and the company, option dealings, directors' service contracts, payments to directors for loss of office, disclosure of directors' personal interest in a contract). In addition, directors can be disqualified in a number of instances, or even asked to contribute personally to the company's assets in the event of wrongful or fraudulent trading. Wrongful trading occurs when your company has gone into insolvent liquidation and at some time before the commencement of the winding up of the company the directors of the company knew or ought to have concluded there was no reasonable prospect that the company would avoid going into insolvent liquidation. If the company continues to trade in these circumstances, the director can be forced to contribute personally to the company's assets.

Company secretary

Your company must have a secretary. The secretary is responsible with the directors for keeping the company's registers and minutes and for filing information at Companies House. The secretary also attends the meetings of directors and shareholders to record the minutes.

The first secretary is appointed on incorporation. The Board can also pass resolutions to appoint or remove a secretary.

CHAPTER 6

The shareholders

What you'll find in this chapter

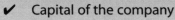

✔ Capital of the company
✔ Transfer of shares
✔ Shareholders' meetings
✔ Written resolutions

Capital of the company

The company consists of one or more shareholders who own shares. A company is incorporated with an authorised share capital. In this *Made Easy* Guide it is £100 and each share has a nominal value of £1.

When a company is incorporated, it issues shares to shareholders. These shares are paid for with money, property or services. If, for example, shareholders applied for two shares and these were issued, you would say that the company had an issued share capital of £2 and an authorised share capital of £100. The directors can issue the remaining 98 composing the authorised share capital. Provided that the shareholders have passed an ordinary resolution to increase the share capital, the directors can issue the shares composing the increased share capital. The authority in the Articles (see Article 7) permits the directors to issue shares up to a maximum nominal amount equal to the authorised share capital.

Note that the authority expires five years after the date of incorporation. If shares are to be allotted for cash, there are statutory rules governing the manner and timing of such an offer which require that shares be offered to existing shareholders, in proportion to their shareholdings. If you want to exclude these rules (e.g. if you want to offer shares to a new shareholder), you should consult a solicitor. In the example company of this Made Easy Guide only one share (in the event of the company being a single-member company) or two shares have been issued.

Shares can be issued at a price greater than their nominal value to bring more money into the company, while protecting the voting rights of existing shareholders and avoiding the procedures required to increase the authorised share capital of the company. For example, £1 shares could be sold for £10 with the difference between the actual and nominal value of each share (£10 − £1 = £9) being held in a separate account, known as a share premium account.

Remember that no private company is allowed to issue or cause to be issued any advertisement offering shares for sale to the public.

Once the directors have issued all the shares in the authorised capital (in the case of this *Made Easy* Guide company £100), no additional shares may be issued unless the share capital is increased by an ordinary resolution of the shareholders. In addition, the shareholders must authorise the directors to allot any shares represented by the increased capital.

In this *Made Easy* Guide the rights attached to the ordinary shares entitle the holders to notice of shareholders' meetings and to speak and vote at such meetings. On a poll each share carries one vote. Shareholders are entitled to any dividends declared by the company and a proportion of the company's assets on dissolution.

The shares may be paid for, nil paid (unpaid) or partly paid for on issue. If they are partly paid for or nil paid, the company will be entitled to ask for the balance owed on each share and the shareholder must pay it.

 Remember that no private company is allowed to issue or cause to be issued any advertisement offering shares for sale to the public.

Transfer of shares

Having issued shares in your company, the shareholders may want to be able to sell their shares or give them away. They may only transfer their shares in accordance with the Articles of Association. The Articles you are provided with require shareholders to appoint the company as their agent for the transfer of shares (see Article 26). The company is obliged to offer the transfer shares to the existing shareholders. If the company fails to find a purchaser among the existing shareholders within 28 days, the selling shareholder is free to sell his shares to outsiders (subject always to the directors' power to refuse to register a transfer of shares). There are provisions for dealing with the negotiation of a fair price for the shares within this clause.

Shareholders' meetings

Most of the day-to-day running of the company is carried out by the directors so you will not need to worry about the following unless it is a very important issue (e.g. issues concerning capital or the company's constitution) which is decided by the shareholders. In some cases, directors and shareholders will be the same people.

 Shareholders act officially as a group. This means that either a formal meeting or a written resolution signed by all the shareholders is necessary before it can legally bind the company. If you do not wish to hold a meeting and want to act by written resolution, use the example format in this Guide.

Shareholders act officially as a group. This means that either a formal meeting or a written resolution signed by all the shareholders is necessary before they can legally bind the company. Please turn to page 41 if you do not wish to hold a meeting and want to act by written resolution.

Certain rules and procedures have to be followed in order to call and conduct a shareholders' meeting:

Notice

Shareholders must receive advance warning of meetings.

1. Each shareholder entitled to attend the meeting must receive notice of all meetings (see Articles 40 and 41). Each should be notified of the date, time and place and full details of the proposed resolution to be considered at the meeting.

2. Each shareholder must receive his own notice of the meeting. The length of notice depends upon the type of resolution proposed.

    a) In the case of an Annual General Meeting or a general meeting at which a special resolution is proposed, at least 21 clear days' notice should be given.

    b) In the case of a general meeting other than an Annual General Meeting or a general meeting at which a special resolution is proposed, at least 14 clear days' notice should be given. An example format of a Notice of an EGM (Extraordinary General Meeting) is included in this *Made Easy* Guide (see page 111).

    c) It is also possible for meetings to be held at short notice provided the requisite majority of shareholders have consented to short notice. This consent is recorded and signed in writing.

    In most cases, you will be able to hold the meeting immediately if you obtain the shareholders' consent to short notice. An example format of a consent to short notice is included in this *Made Easy* Guide (see page 112).

    Consent to short notice may be given:

    (i) in the case of an Annual General Meeting, by all the members entitled to attend and vote at the meeting; and

    (ii) in the case of general meetings, by a majority in number of the members holding not less than 95 per cent in nominal value of the shares and having the right to attend and vote at the meeting (or 90 per cent if an elective resolution to that effect has been passed).

Proxies

Each shareholder may appoint someone to attend the meeting on his behalf (a proxy) if he is unable to attend. The proxy may attend and speak at the meeting and vote on a poll on the shareholder's behalf (see Articles 61–65). The proxy may not vote on a show of hands.

The notice calling the meeting should inform shareholders that they are entitled to appoint a proxy to attend and vote in their place and that the proxy need not be a shareholder.

The proxy form must be lodged with the company within a specified period before the meeting is held (this period cannot be longer than 48 hours). See Article 62 or 63 for a proxy form.

Quorum

Shareholders act collectively, not individually, so a certain number of shareholders must be present before a meeting can be held. This is known as a 'quorum'. Article 42 provides for a minimum of two shareholders present either in person or by proxy to be a quorum; in the event of the company only having one shareholder, he will form a quorum. Resolutions are passed by a majority of the shareholders at shareholders' meetings. The example company in this *Made Easy* Guide has one or two shareholders and does not provide the chairperson with a casting vote (i.e. a second vote in addition to his shareholder's vote). Should your company grow and the number of shareholders increase, you may want to amend your Articles to include a chairperson's casting vote to avoid a possible impasse at shareholders' meetings.

Voting

Shareholders vote to make their collective decisions. The vote, which takes place at the meeting, can be made in one of two ways:

- **On a show of hands** – every shareholder present in person is entitled to cast one vote. Proxies are not entitled to vote.

- **On a poll** – every shareholder present shall be entitled to cast one vote for every share held. Proxies can vote on a poll. For how a poll can be demanded see Article 48.

The number of votes required to pass a particular item depends on whether the resolution is ordinary or special.

1. Ordinary resolutions

Ordinary resolutions proposed at a general meeting must be approved by a simple majority (i.e. more than 50 per cent) of the votes cast at the meeting, whether by a show of hands or on a poll. Examples of business which must be approved by ordinary resolution include:

a) Increasing the share capital. You also must file Form 123 at Companies House.

b) Removal of a director.

There are many more instances when an ordinary resolution is required. Those instances are not covered here. The above is merely to give you an example of the sort of business which is transacted by shareholders rather than by directors.

2. Special resolutions

Special resolutions must be passed by a three-quarters majority of the votes cast at the meeting, whether by a show of hands or on a poll.

Examples of business which must be approved by special resolution are:

a) Alteration to Memorandum of Association.

b) Alteration to the Articles of Association.

c) Reduction of capital.

d) A change of name. You also must send the appropriate fee to Companies House.

There are many more instances when a special resolution is required. Those instances are not covered here.

Some ordinary and all special resolutions must be filed at Companies House within 15 days of being passed (see page 114). Sometimes forms and fees must also accompany the resolutions (e.g. Form 123).

Written resolutions

It is possible (and less complicated) for the shareholders to pass a written resolution provided it is signed by or on behalf of all shareholders entitled to attend and vote at the meeting. No notice of the proposed resolution is required. This is the simplest way of transacting business and avoids the necessity of a meeting. An example format of written resolutions appears on pages 115–16.

Written resolutions which would not have been effective unless passed as special resolutions and some other written resolutions must be filed at Companies House within 15 days of being passed.

CHAPTER 7

Post-incorporation changes

What you'll find in this chapter

✔ Appointment or removal of the company secretary
✔ Appointment or removal of auditors
✔ Location of the registered office
✔ The name of the company
✔ Increase in company capital
✔ Allotting shares
✔ The objects clause
✔ The Articles of Association
✔ The accounting reference date

It is possible to make changes to the corporate structure after you have successfully set up your company. However, there are strict procedural formalities that must be followed. Companies House must always be kept informed of corporate changes; failure to file the proper documentation will result in penalties.

The most common post-incorporation changes involve:

Appointment or removal of the company secretary

This decision is made by the company directors. It is not necessary for the shareholders to vote on this issue, but Companies House must be notified of any change.

Appointment or removal of auditors

Normally, an auditor is appointed at the Annual General Meeting and serves until the next such meeting. If the auditor decides to resign, he must deposit notice with the company, indicating whether there are circumstances that ought to be drawn to the attention of members or creditors of the company (or not), and the company must deposit such notice with Companies House. If there are circumstances which the auditor considers should be drawn to the attention of members or creditors, a copy of the auditor's statement must be sent to each member or the company applies to court. The resigning auditor may also require the company to convene an Extraordinary General Meeting to provide his comments to members, and can require the company to circulate his written comments in advance of the meeting.

A company may remove an auditor from office by an ordinary resolution. If the resolution is to be proposed before the expiry of the auditor's term of office or to appoint an auditor other than a retiring auditor, special notice needs to be given by a member of his intention to propose such a resolution. Notice must be given to the auditor whom it is proposed to remove and to the person whom it is proposed to appoint. An auditor proposed to be removed or retiring without being proposed for re-appointment is entitled to make written representations to the company and to have these circulated to members or read out at the general meeting. If the company is contemplating changing auditors or removing an auditor from office, legal advice should be obtained to ensure all the necessary formalities are observed.

Location of the registered office

If the company wants to change the location of the registered office, or of the statutory books and other documents open to the public, Companies House must be notified within 14 days of the change.

The name of the company

A majority of shareholders must vote for a special resolution to change the name of the company. This special resolution must be filed with Companies House within 15 days of the meeting.

Increase in company capital

A company can increase its authorised share capital by an ordinary resolution passed at a general meeting or through the passing of a member's written resolution. On an increase in capital, the directors will be unable to allot the newly created shares unless authority is conferred on them (by ordinary resolution) to allot such shares (see 'Allotting shares' below). Within 15 days of the passing of the resolution by the company, a notice (on Form G123) must be delivered to Companies House together with a copy of the revised Memorandum.

Allotting shares

Altering directors' authority to allot shares requires a majority adoption of an ordinary resolution at a general meeting. A copy of that resolution must be sent to Companies House within 15 days of its adoption.

The objects clause

If the company desires to change its objects clause and thus its Memorandum of Association, 75 per cent of the shareholders must agree to a special resolution.

The Articles of Association

The Articles of Association may be altered by a majority of 75 per cent of the shareholders voting on a special resolution.

The accounting reference date

If a change is made to the accounting reference date, details of the change must be submitted to Companies House before the end of the accounting period.

Glossary

Accounting reference date	The annual anniversary upon which the company's financial year ends.
Accounting reference period	The period which ends on the accounting reference date.
Allotment	The appropriation by the Board of shares in the capital of the company to the holders of shares.
Articles of Association	The document containing the company's regulations for its internal management.
Assets	Anything owned of monetary value, including both real and personal property.
Authorised capital	The nominal capital which the company is authorised to issue by its Memorandum of Association. This capital may be increased by subsequent resolution.
Board	The collective term for the directors of the company who determine and carry out company policy.
Board meeting	A meeting of the directors at which a quorum is present.
Clear days	The period of notice to be given to a member of the company of a general meeting which excludes the day the notice is served on the member, usually 48 hours after posting and the day of the meeting.
Director	An officer of the company who manages the business conducted by the company.

Elective resolution	A resolution that a private company is entitled to pass to reduce or remove certain administrative or formal requirements and requiring the consent of all those shareholders entitled to vote.
General meeting	An Annual General Meeting or an Extraordinary General Meeting, where shareholders give their approval for transactions.
Incorporate	To form a limited company by following procedures prescribed by law. On incorporation the limited company becomes a separate legal entity in its own right distinct from its owners.
Issued shares	The number of shares issued by the company to its shareholders.
Member	Someone who is a subscriber or who has agreed to become a member of the company and whose name is entered in the Register of Members.
Memorandum of Association	The company's charter defining the extent of the company's powers.
Minutes	Written records of formal proceedings of shareholders' and directors' meetings.
Poll	Ascertaining the will of the shareholders at a general meeting of the company by counting shareholders' votes according to the size of their shareholding. On a poll a proxy may vote.
Pre-emption	The right of existing shareholders granting them first option to acquire shares which are to be transferred or issued in proportion to their present shareholding.
Proxy	Shareholder's authorisation appointing another to attend a meeting to speak and vote on his behalf. A proxy may also be the person so authorised.
Quorum	The number of shareholders or directors who must be present before a meeting can be held.
Registered office	The postal address of the company notified to Companies House for the receipt of legal documents and other official correspondence.

Resolution	Decision made by directors or shareholders in accordance with requisite majorities set out in Articles of Association. Resolutions are approved in meetings or in writing.
Share certificate	Written and executed instrument showing who holds title to a particular share or series of shares.
Shareholder	Someone who holds shares in the company.
Statutory books	The records that a company must keep as required by law. Changes must be notified to the Registrar of Companies at Companies House. These records are available for public inspection.
Subscriber	A person who signs the Memorandum of Association.
Written resolution	A resolution passed by either the shareholders or the directors of the company by signing a written form of the resolution rather than being at a general meeting of the company or at a meeting of the directors of the company.

List of sensitive words

The use of a company or business name that includes any of the following words will require the approval of the Secretary of State for Trade and Industry.

Association
Assurance
Assurer
Authority
Benevolent
Board
British
Chamber(s) of Commerce
Chamber(s) of Trade
Charter
Chartered
Chemist
Chemistry
Co-operative
Council
England
English
European
Federation
Foundation

Friendly Society	
Fund	
Great Britain	
Group	
Holding	
Industrial & Provident Society	
Institute	
Institution	
Insurance	
Insurer	
International	
Ireland	
Irish	
National	
Patent	
Patentee	
Post Office	
Reassurance	
Reassurer	
Register	
Registered	
Reinsurance	
Reinsurer	
Scotland	
Scottish	
Sheffield	
Society	
Stock Exchange	
Trade Union	
Trust	
United Kingdom	
Wales	
Welsh	

The use of a company or business name which includes any of the following words or expressions requires the Secretary of State's approval (see chapter 3). A written request must be made seeking the opinion of the relevant body as to the use of the word or expression. A copy of any response received will be required by Companies House before approval is sought from the Secretary of State.

Word or expression	Relevant body in England and Wales	Relevant body in Scotland
Charitable, Charity	Head of Status *Charity Commission* Woodfield House Tangier Taunton TA1 4BL	*For recognition as a Scottish charity: Inland Revenue FICO (Scotland)* Trinity Park House South Trinity Road Edinburgh EH5 3SD
Contact Lens	The Registrar *General Optical Council* 41 Harley Street London W1N 2DJ	As for England and Wales
Dental, Dentistry	The Registrar *General Dental Council* 37 Wimpole Street London W1M 8DQ	As for England and Wales
Nurse, District Nurse, Health Visitor, Midwife, Midwifery, Nursing	The Registrar & Chief Executive *UK Central Council for Nursing, Midwifery and Health Visiting* 23 Portland Place London W1N 3AF	As for England and Wales
Health Centre	Office of the Solicitor *Department of Health & Social Security* 48 Carey Street London WC2A 2LS	As for England and Wales

Word or expression	Relevant body in England and Wales	Relevant body in Scotland
Health Service	*Department of Health* Room 2N35A Quarry House Quarry Hill Leeds LS2 7UE	As for England and Wales
Police	*Home Office* Police Department Strategy Group Room 510 50 Queen Anne's Gate London SW1H 9AT	*The Scottish Ministers* Police Division St Andrews House Regent Road Edinburgh EH1 3DG
Polytechnic	*Department for Education and Science* FHE 1B Sanctuary Buildings Great Smith Street Westminster London SW1P 3BT	As for England and Wales
Pregnancy, Abortion, Termination	*Department of Health* Area 423 Wellington House 133–155 Waterloo Road London SE1 8UG	As for England and Wales
	If based in England:	
Royal, Duke, His/Her Majesty, King, Prince, Princess, Queen, Royale, Royalty, Windsor	*Lord Chancellor's Dept* Constitutional Policy Division 1st Floor, Southside 105 Victoria Street London SW1E 6QT	*The Scottish Ministers* Civil Law and Legal Aid Division Saughton House Broomhouse Drive Edinburgh EH1 3XD

Word or expression	Relevant body in England and Wales	Relevant body in Scotland
	If based in Wales: *The National Assembly for Wales* Crown Buildings Cathays Park Cardiff CF1 3NQ	
Special School	*Department for Education and Employment* Schools 2 Branch Sanctuary Buildings Great Smith Street Westminster London SW1P 3BT	As for England and Wales
University	*Privy Council Office* 2 Carlton Gardens London SW1Y 5AA	As for England and Wales

The use of certain words in company or business names is covered by other legislation and their use may constitute a criminal offence. Some of these words are listed below, but the list is not exhaustive. Owners of a business wishing to use any of these words should obtain confirmation from the appropriate body that the use of the word does not contravene the relevant legislation.

Word or expression	Relevant legislation	Relevant body
Anzac	s1 Anzac Act 1916	Seek advice from *Companies House*
Architect	s20 Architects Act 1997	*Architects Registration Board* 73 Hallam Street London W1N 6EE

Word or expression	Relevant legislation	Relevant body
Building Society	Building Society Act 1986	Seek advice from *Building Societies Commission* Victoria House 30-40 Kingsway London WC2B 6ES
Chamber(s) of Business, Chamber(s) of Commerce, Chamber(s) of Commerce and Industry, Chamber(s) of Commerce Training and Enterprise, Chamber(s) of Enterprise, Chamber(s) of Industry Chamber(s) of Trade, Chamber(s) of Trade and Industry, Chamber(s) of Training, Chamber(s) of Training and Enterprise, or the Welsh translations of these words	Company and Business Names (Chamber of Commerce etc.) Act 1999	Seek guidance from *Companies House*
Chiropodist, Dietician, Medical Laboratory Technician, Occupational Therapist, Orthoptist, Physiotherapist, Radiographer, Remedial Gymnast	Professions Supplementary to Medicine Act 1960 if preceded by Registered, State or Registered	*Department of Health* HRD HRB Room 2N35A Quarry House Quarry Hill Leeds LS2 7UE

Word or expression	Relevant legislation	Relevant body
Credit Union	Credit Unions Act 1979	The Public Records Section *Financial Services Authority* 25 The North Colonnade Canary Wharf London E14 5HS
Dental Practitioner, Dental Surgeon, Dentist	Dentists Act 1984	The Registrar *General Dental Council* 37 Wimpole Street London W1M 8DQ
Drug, Druggist, Pharmaceutical, Pharmaceutist, Pharmacist, Pharmacy	s78 Medicines Act 1968	The Director of Legal Services *Royal Pharmaceutical Society of Great Britain* Law Department 1 Lambeth High Street London SE1 7JN If based in Scotland: *Pharmaceutical Society of Great Britain* 36 York Place Edinburgh EH1 3HU
Institute of Laryngology, Institute of Orthopaedics, Institute of Otology, Institute of Urology	University College London Act 1988	Seek advice from *University College London* Gower Street London WC1E 6BT

Word or expression	Relevant legislation	Relevant body
Olympiad, Olympiads, Olympian, Olympians, Olympic, Olympics or translation of these	Olympic Symbol etc. (Protection) Act 1995* *Also protects Olympic symbols of five interlocking rings and motto 'Citius Altius Fortius'*	*British Olympic Association* 1 Wandsworth Plain London SW18 1EH
Optician, Dispensing Optician, Enrolled Optician, Ophthalmic Optician, Optometrist, Registered Optician	Opticians Act 1989	The Registrar *General Optical Council* 41 Harley Street London W1N 2DJ
Patent Agent, Patent Office	Copyright, Designs and Patents Act 1988	*IPPD (Intellectual Property Policy Directorate)* Room 3B38 Concept House The Patent Office Cardiff Road Newport NP10 8QQ
Red Cross, Geneva Cross, Red Crescent, Red Lion and Sun	Geneva Convention Act 1957	Seek advice from *Companies House*
Solicitors (Scotland)	s31 Solicitors (Scotland) Act 1980	*Law Society of Scotland* 26 Drumsheugh Gardens Edinburgh EH3 7YR
Vet, Veterinary, Veterinary Surgeon	s19/20 Veterinary Surgeons Act 1966	The Registrar *Royal College of Veterinary Surgeons* 62–64 Horseferry Road London SW1P 2AF

APPENDIX
Example forms

These forms are available to download from Lawpack's website at www.lawpack.co.uk:

Memorandum of Association   61

Articles of Association   63

Share Certificate   94

Completed examples of forms, which are also available to download from our website:

Form 10: First directors and secretary and intended situation of registered office   96

Form 12: Declaration on application for registration   100

Form G88(2): Return of allotment of shares   101

Form 123: Notice of increase in nominal capital   103

Form 225: Change of accounting reference date   104

Example formats to help you prepare your own documents:

Minutes of the First Meeting of the Directors   105

Written Resolution of All the Directors   107

Registers   109

Notice of Extraordinary General Meeting 111

Consent to Short Notice of Extraordinary General Meeting 112

Minutes of Extraordinary General Meeting 113

Ordinary and Special Resolutions 114

Elective Resolutions Passed as Written Shareholders' Resolutions 115

 When downloading these forms from our website, please remember that Companies House requires them to be printed on A4 size, plain white paper at 80–100gsm in weight with a matt finish. It advises that you do not use a dot matrix printer. For more information on its requirements, please go to www.companies house.gov.uk/about/pdf/gb01.pdf.

Memorandum of Association

The Companies Acts 1985 to 1989
Private Company Limited by Shares

MEMORANDUM OF ASSOCIATION OF

LIMITED

1. The company's name is '   Limited'.

2. The company's registered office is to be situated in England and Wales/ Scotland.

3. The object of the company is to carry on business as a general commercial company.

4. The liability of the members is limited.

5. The company's share capital is £100 divided into 100 shares of £1 each.

I/We*, the subscriber(s) to this Memorandum of Association, wish to be formed into a company pursuant to this Memorandum; and I/we* agree to take the number of shares shown opposite my/our* respective name(s).

Signature(s), name(s) and
address(es) of subscriber(s):

Number of shares taken by
each subscriber:

1. Signature _____

    Name   _____   _____

    Address   _____

               _____

2. Signature _____

    Name   _____   _____

    Address   _____

               _____

Total shares taken   _____

Dated this _____ day of _____ year _____

Witness to the above signature   Signature _____

                                      Name   _____

                                      Address   _____

                                                  _____

* Delete as appropriate

Example Memorandum of Association

The Companies Acts 1985 to 1989
Private Company Limited by Shares

MEMORANDUM OF ASSOCIATION OF
Lawpack Publishing LIMITED

1. The company's name is 'Lawpack Publishing Limited'.

2. The company's registered office is to be situated in England and Wales/ ~~Scotland~~.

3. The object of the company is to carry on business as a general commercial company.

4. The liability of the members is limited.

5. The company's share capital is £100 divided into 100 shares of £1 each.

~~I~~/We*, the subscriber(s) to this Memorandum of Association, wish to be formed into a company pursuant to this Memorandum; and ~~I~~/we* agree to take the number of shares shown opposite ~~my~~/our* respective name(s).

Signature(s), name(s) and address(es) of subscriber(s):	Number of shares taken by each subscriber:
1. Signature *A Palmer*	
Name Alexander Palmer	One
Address 85 Preston Square	
London SW6 5CN	
2. Signature *Julia Etheridge*	
Name Julia Etheridge	One
Address 16 St. George's Crescent	
Reading RG7 9XY	
Total shares taken	Two

Dated this __3__ day of _____January_____ year _2005_

Witness to the above signature Signature *Adam Bennett*

Name Adam Bennett

Address 32 Church Grove

London SW6 6RW

* Delete as appropriate

Articles of Association

The Companies Acts 1985 to 1989
Private Company Limited by Shares

ARTICLES OF ASSOCIATION OF

LIMITED

1. The provisions of Table A as contained in the Companies (Tables A to F) Regulations shall be excluded in whole from applying to the Company.

Interpretation

2. In these articles –

'the Act' means the Companies Act 1985 including any statutory modification or re-enactment thereof for the time being in force.

'the articles' means these articles.

'clear days' in relation to the period of a notice means that period excluding the day when the notice is given or deemed to be given and the day for which it is given or on which it is to take effect.

'communication' means the same as in the Electronic Communications Act 2000.

'electronic communication' means the same as in the Electronic Communications Act 2000.

'executed' includes any mode of execution.

'office' means the registered office of the company.

'the holder' in relation to shares means the member whose name is entered in the register of members as the holder of the shares.

'the seal' means the common seal of the company.

'secretary' means the secretary of the company or any other person appointed to perform the duties of the secretary of the company, including a joint, assistant or deputy secretary.

'the United Kingdom' means Great Britain and Northern Ireland.

Unless the context otherwise requires, words or expressions contained in these articles bear the same meaning as in the Act but excluding any

Articles of Association (continued)

statutory modification thereof not in force when these articles become binding on the company.

Share capital

3. Subject to the provisions of the Act and without prejudice to any rights attached to any existing shares, any share may be issued with such rights or restrictions as the company may by ordinary resolution determine.

4. Subject to the provisions of the Act, shares may be issued which are to be redeemed or are to be liable to be redeemed at the option of the company or the holder on such terms and in such manner as may be provided by the articles.

5. The company may exercise the powers of paying commissions conferred by the Act. Subject to the provisions of the Act, any such commission may be satisfied by the payment of cash or by the allotment of fully or partly paid shares or partly in one way and partly in the other.

6. Except as required by law, no person shall be recognised by the company as holding any share upon any trust and (except as otherwise provided by the articles or by law) the company shall not be bound by or recognise any interest in any share except an absolute right to the entirety thereof in the holder.

7. The directors are generally and unconditionally authorised for the purposes of section 80 of the Companies Act 1985 to allot and grant rights to subscribe for or to convert securities into shares of the company to such persons at such times and generally upon such terms and conditions as the directors may determine up to the authorised share capital with which the company is incorporated from the date of incorporation of the company at any time or times during the period of five years from this date, and the directors may after the expiry of this period allot any shares or grant any rights under this authority in pursuance of any offer or agreement made within that period.

Share certificates

8. Every member, upon becoming the holder of any shares, shall be entitled without payment to one certificate for all the shares of each class held by him (and, upon transferring a part of his holding of shares of any class, to

Articles of Association (continued)

a certificate for the balance of such holding) or several certificates each for one or more of his shares upon payment for every certificate after the first of such reasonable sum as the directors may determine. Every certificate shall be sealed with the seal (if the company has a seal) and shall specify the number, class and distinguishing numbers (if any) of the shares to which it relates and the amount or respective amounts paid up thereon. The company shall not be bound to issue more than one certificate for shares held jointly by several persons and delivery of a certificate to one joint holder shall be a sufficient delivery to all of them.

9. If a share certificate is defaced, worn-out, lost or destroyed, it may be renewed on such terms (if any) as to evidence and indemnity and payment of the expenses reasonably incurred by the company in investigating evidence as the directors may determine but otherwise free of charge, and (in the case of defacement or wearing-out) on delivery up of the old certificate.

Lien

10. The company shall have a first and paramount lien on every share (not being a fully paid share) for all moneys (whether presently payable or not) payable at a fixed time or called in respect of that share. The directors may at any time declare any share to be wholly or in part exempt from the provisions of this article. The company's lien on a share shall extend to any amount payable in respect of it.

11. The company may sell in such manner as the directors determine any shares on which the company has a lien if a sum in respect of which the lien exists is presently payable and is not paid within fourteen clear days after notice has been given to the holder of the share or to the person entitled to it in consequence of the death or bankruptcy of the holder, demanding payment and stating that if the notice is not complied with the shares may be sold.

12. To give effect to a sale the directors may authorise some person to execute an instrument of transfer of the shares sold to, or in accordance with the directions of, the purchaser. The title of the transferee to the shares shall not be affected by any irregularity in or invalidity of the proceedings in reference to the sale.

Articles of Association (continued)

13. The net proceeds of the sale, after payment of the costs, shall be applied in payment of so much of the sum for which the lien exists as is presently payable, and any residue shall (upon surrender to the company for cancellation of the certificate for the shares sold and subject to a like lien for any moneys not presently payable as existed upon the shares before the sale) be paid to the person entitled to the shares at the date of the sale.

Calls on shares and forfeiture

14. Subject to the terms of allotment, the directors may make calls upon the members in respect of any moneys unpaid on their shares (whether in respect of nominal value or premium) and each member shall (subject to receiving at least fourteen clear days' notice specifying when and where payment is to be made) pay to the company as required by the notice the amount called on his shares. A call may be required to be paid by instalments. A call may, before receipt by the company of any sum due thereunder, be revoked in whole or part and payment of a call may be postponed in whole or part. A person upon whom a call is made shall remain liable for calls made upon him notwithstanding the subsequent transfer of the shares in respect whereof the call was made.

15. A call shall be deemed to have been made at the time when the resolution of the directors authorising the call was passed.

16. The joint holders of a share shall be jointly and severally liable to pay all calls in respect thereof.

17. If a call remains unpaid after it has become due and payable the person from whom it is due and payable shall pay interest on the amount unpaid from the day it became due and payable until it is paid at the rate fixed by the terms of allotment of the share or in the notice of the call, or if no rate is fixed, at the appropriate rate (as defined by the Act) but the directors may waive payment of the interest wholly or in part.

18. An amount payable in respect of a share on allotment or at any fixed date, whether in respect of nominal value or premium or as an instalment of a call, shall be deemed to be a call and if not paid the provisions of the articles shall apply as if that amount had become due and payable by virtue of a call.

Articles of Association (continued)

19. Subject to the terms of allotment, the directors may make arrangements on the issue of shares for a difference between the holders in the amounts and times of payment of calls on their shares.

20. If a call remains unpaid after it has become due and payable the directors may give to the person from whom it is due not less than fourteen clear days' notice requiring payment of the amount unpaid together with any interest which may have accrued. The notice shall name the place where payment is to be made and shall state that if the notice is not complied with the shares in respect of which the call was made will be liable to be forfeited.

21. If the notice is not complied with any share in respect of which it was given may, before the payment required by the notice has been made, be forfeited by a resolution of the directors and the forfeiture shall include all dividends or other moneys payable in respect of the forfeited shares and not paid before the forfeiture.

22. Subject to the provisions of the Act, a forfeited share may be sold, re-allotted or otherwise disposed of on such terms and in such manner as the directors determine either to the person who was before the forfeiture the holder or to any other person and at any time before sale, re-allotment or other disposition, the forfeiture may be cancelled on such terms as the directors think fit. Where for the purposes of its disposal a forfeited share is to be transferred to any person the directors may authorise some person to execute an instrument of transfer of the share to that person.

23. A person any of whose shares have been forfeited shall cease to be a member in respect of them and shall surrender to the company for cancellation the certificate for the shares forfeited but shall remain liable to the company for all moneys which at the date of forfeiture where presently payable by him to the company in respect of those shares with interest at the rate at which interest was payable on those moneys before the forfeiture or, if no interest was so payable, at the appropriate rate (as defined in the Act) from the date of forfeiture until payment but the directors may waive payment wholly or in part or enforce payment without any allowance for the value of the shares at the time of forfeiture or for any consideration received on their disposal.

Articles of Association (continued)

24. A statutory declaration by a director or the secretary that a share has been forfeited on a specified date shall be conclusive evidence of the facts stated in it as against all persons claiming to be entitled to the share and the declaration shall (subject to the execution of an instrument of transfer if necessary) constitute a good title to the share and the person to whom the share is disposed of shall not be bound to see to the application of the consideration, if any, nor shall his title to the share be affected by any irregularity in or invalidity of the proceedings in reference to the forfeiture or disposal of the share.

Transfer of shares

25. The instrument of transfer of a share may be in any usual form or in any other form which the directors may approve and shall be executed by or on behalf of the transferor and, unless the share is fully paid, by or on behalf of the transferee.

26. (a) (i) A person whether a member of the company or not ('the proposing transferor') proposing to transfer any shares shall give a notice in writing (a 'transfer notice') to the company that he desires to transfer such shares, and the transfer notice shall constitute the company his agent for the sale of all (but not a part only) of the shares specified in the notice to any member or members at the prescribed price (as defined below). A transfer notice once received by the company shall not be revocable without the prior consent of the directors;

    (ii) If within a period of 28 days after receiving a transfer notice the company finds a member or members ('the purchaser') willing to purchase all the shares specified in the transfer notice the company shall give written notice of the fact to the proposing transferor and he shall be bound upon payment of the prescribed price to transfer those shares to the purchaser;

    (iii) Every notice given by the company under the preceding paragraph stating that it has found a purchaser for the shares specified in the transfer notice shall state the name and address of the purchaser and the number of shares which he has agreed to purchase. The purchase shall be completed at a place and

Articles of Association (continued)

time to be appointed by the company, not being more than 28 days after the prescribed price shall have been agreed or determined under paragraph 25 (a)(vi) of this article. For the purpose of determining the right to any distribution by the company, the proposing transferor shall be deemed to have sold such shares on the date of the notice so given by the company;

(iv) If the proposing transferor, after having become bound to transfer any shares to a purchaser, fails to do so, the directors may authorise some person to sign an instrument of transfer on behalf of the proposing transferor in favour of the purchaser, and the company may receive the purchase money, and shall at that time cause the name of the purchaser to be entered in the register as the holder of the shares and shall hold the purchase money in trust for the proposing transferor. The receipt of the company for the purchase money shall be a good discharge to the purchaser, who shall not be bound to see to its application; and after his name has been entered in the register the validity of the proceedings shall not be questioned by any person;

(v) If within a period of 28 days after receiving a transfer notice ('the prescribed period') the company shall not find purchasers for all the shares specified in the transfer notice, and gives notice in writing to that effect to the proposing transferor, or if the company within the prescribed period gives to the proposing transferor notice in writing that it has no prospect of finding such purchasers, the proposing transferor shall be at liberty, until the expiration of four months after the end of the prescribed period, to transfer all or any of the shares specified in the transfer notice to any person and at any price, or by way of gift; provided that, if the directors shall so resolve, the company may when giving notice under this paragraph inform the proposing transferor that the company will, subject to and in accordance with the provisions of chapter VII of part V of the Act, as soon as practicable purchase all the shares specified in the transfer notice at the prescribed price, and such notice shall be binding upon the company and the proposing transferor, who shall respectively take all steps within their power for carrying such purchase into effect;

(vi) if within one month after the receipt by the proposing transferor of a notice given by the company under paragraph 25(a)(ii) of this article he shall have agreed with the purchaser a price per share for any shares then that price shall be the prescribed price of those shares. For any other shares, the auditors for the time being of the company or (if the proposing transferor shall so request or if the company satisfies the requirements for audit exemption and has no auditors) some other chartered accountant nominated by the President of the Institute of Chartered Accountants in England and Wales or Scotland (dependant on the country of incorporation) shall determine the fair value of such shares, the value so determined being the prescribed price for those shares and in determining the prescribed price they or he shall have power to determine how the costs of fixing it shall be borne. In making the determination the auditors or the chartered accountant nominated by the President of the Institute of Chartered Accountants shall act as an expert and not as an arbitrator and their or his determination shall be final and binding;

(vii) all shares comprised in any transfer notice shall be offered by the company in the first instance for sale at the prescribed price to all members holding shares of the same class as those so comprised (other than the proposing transferor) on the terms that in case of competition the shares so offered shall be sold to the members accepting the offer in proportion (as nearly as may be) to their existing holdings of such shares. All offers of shares under this paragraph shall be made in writing and sent by prepaid post to the members at their respective registered addresses, and shall limit a time (not being less than 21 days) within which the offer must be accepted or in default will be treated as declined.

(b) The directors may in their absolute discretion and without assigning any reason therefore decline to register any transfer of any share

Articles of Association (continued)

including any transfer which would otherwise be permitted under the preceding provisions of this article.

27. If the directors refuse to register a transfer of a share, they shall within two months after the date on which the transfer was lodged with the company send to the transferee notice of the refusal.

28. The registration of transfers of shares or of transfers of any class of shares may be suspended at such times and for such periods (not exceeding thirty days in any year) as the directors may determine.

29. No fee shall be charged for the registration of any instrument of transfer or other document relating to or affecting the title to any share.

30. The company shall be entitled to retain any instrument of transfer which is registered, but any instrument of transfer which the directors refuse to register shall be returned to the person lodging it when notice of the refusal is given.

Transmission of shares

31. If a member dies the survivor or survivors where he was a joint holder, and his personal representatives where he was a sole holder or the only survivor of joint holders, shall be the only persons recognised by the company as having any title to his interest; but nothing herein contained shall release the estate of a deceased member from any liability in respect of any share which had been jointly held by him.

32. A person becoming entitled to a share in consequence of the death or bankruptcy of a member may, upon such evidence being produced as the directors may properly require, elect either to become the holder of the share or to have some person nominated by him registered as the transferee. If he elects to become the holder he shall give notice to the company to that effect. If he elects to have another person registered he shall execute an instrument of transfer of the share to that person. All the articles relating to the transfer of shares shall apply to the notice or instrument of transfer as if it were an instrument of transfer executed by the member and the death or bankruptcy of the member had not occurred.

33. A person becoming entitled to a share in consequence of the death or

Articles of Association (continued)

bankruptcy of a member shall have the rights to which he would be entitled if he were the holder of the share, except that he shall not, before being registered as the holder of the share, be entitled in respect of it to attend or vote at any meeting of the company or at any separate meeting of the holders of any class of shares in the company.

Alteration of share capital

34. The company may by ordinary resolution –

(a) increase its share capital by new shares of such amount as the resolution prescribes;

(b) consolidate and divide all or any of its share capital into shares of larger amount than its existing shares;

(c) subject to the provision of the Act, sub-divide its shares, or any of them, into shares of smaller amounts and the resolution may determine that, as between the shares resulting from the sub-division, any of them may have any preference or advantage as compared with the others; and

(d) cancel shares which, at the date of the passing of the resolution, have not been taken or agreed to be taken by any person and diminish the amount of its share capital by the amount of the shares so cancelled.

35. Whenever as a result of a consolidation of shares any members would become entitled to fractions of a share, the directors may, on behalf of those members, sell the shares representing the fractions for the best price reasonably obtainable to any person (including, subject to the provisions of the Act, the company) and distribute the net proceeds of sale in due proportion among those members, and the directors may authorise some person to execute an instrument of transfer of the shares to, or in accordance with the direction of, the purchaser. The transferee shall not be bound to see to the application of the purchase money nor shall his title to the shares be affected by any irregularity in or invalidity of the proceedings in reference to the sale.

36. Subject to the provisions of the Act, the company may by special resolution reduce its share capital, any capital redemption reserve and any share premium account in any way.

Articles of Association (continued)

Purchase of own shares

37. Subject to the provisions of the Act, the company may purchase its own shares (including any redeemable shares) and, if it is a private company, make a payment in respect of the redemption or purchase of its own shares otherwise than out of distributable profits of the company or the proceeds of a fresh issue of shares.

General meetings

38. All general meetings other than annual general meetings shall be called extraordinary general meetings.

39. The directors may call general meetings and, on the requisition of members pursuant to the provisions of the Act, shall forthwith proceed to convene an extraordinary general meeting for a date not later than eight weeks after receipt of the requisition. If there are not within the United Kingdom sufficient directors to call a general meeting, any director or any member of the company may call a general meeting.

Notice of general meetings

40. An annual general meeting and an extraordinary general meeting called for the passing of a special resolution or a resolution appointing a person as a director shall be called by at least twenty-one clear days' notice. All other extraordinary general meetings shall be called by at least fourteen clear days' notice but a general meeting may be called by shorter notice if it is so agreed –

(a) in the case of an annual general meeting, by all the members entitled to attend and vote thereat; and

(b) in the case of any other meeting by a majority in number of the members having a right to attend and vote being a majority together holding not less than ninety-five per cent in nominal value of the shares giving that right.

The notice shall specify the time and place of the meeting and the general nature of the business to be transacted and, in the case of an annual general meeting, shall specify the meeting as such.

Subject to the provisions of the articles and to any restrictions imposed on

Articles of Association (continued)

any shares, the notice shall be given to all the members, to all persons entitled to a share in consequence of the death or bankruptcy of a member and to the directors and auditors.

41. The accidental omission to give notice of a meeting to, or the non-receipt of notice of a meeting by, any person entitled to receive notice shall not invalidate the proceedings at that meeting.

Proceedings at general meetings

42. No business shall be transacted at any meeting unless a quorum is present. Two persons entitled to vote upon the business to be transacted, each being a member or a proxy for a member or a duly authorised representative of a corporation, shall be a quorum. If and for so long as the company has only one member that member present in person or by proxy or if a limited company by a duly appointed corporate representative shall be a quorum. If and for so long as the company has only one member and that person takes any decision which is required to be taken in a general meeting or by means of a members' written resolution that decision shall be as valid and effectual as if agreed by the company in a general meeting and any decision of the sole member shall be recorded in writing and delivered to the company for entry in the minute book.

43. If such a quorum is not present within half an hour from the time appointed for the meeting, or if during a meeting such a quorum ceases to be present, the meeting shall stand adjourned to the same day in the next week at the same time and place or to such time and place as the directors may determine.

44. The chairman, if any, of the board of directors or in his absence some other director nominated by the directors shall preside as chairman of the meeting, but if neither the chairman nor such other director (if any) be present within fifteen minutes after the time appointed for holding the meeting and willing to act, the directors present shall elect one of their number to be chairman and, if there is only one director present and willing to act, he shall be chairman.

45. If no director is willing to act as chairman, or if no director is present

Articles of Association (continued)

within fifteen minutes after the time appointed for holding the meeting, the members present and entitled to vote shall choose one of their number to be chairman.

46. A director shall, notwithstanding that he is not a member, be entitled to attend and speak at any general meeting and at any separate meeting of the holders of any class of shares in the company.

47. The chairman may, with the consent of a meeting at which a quorum is present (and shall if so directed by the meeting), adjourn the meeting from time to time and from place to place, but no business shall be transacted at an adjourned meeting other than business which might properly have been transacted at the meeting had the adjournment not taken place. When a meeting is adjourned for fourteen days or more, at least seven clear days' notice shall be given specifying the time and place of the adjourned meeting and the general nature of the business to be transacted. Otherwise it shall not be necessary to give any such notice.

48. A resolution put to the vote of a meeting shall be decided on a show of hands unless before, or on the declaration of the result of, the show of hands a poll is duly demanded. Subject to the provisions of the Act, a poll may be demanded –

    (a) by the chairman; or

    (b) by at least two members having the right to vote at the meeting; or

    (c) by a member or members representing not less than one-tenth of the total voting rights of all the members having the right to vote at the meeting; or

    (d) by a member or members holding shares conferring a right to vote at the meeting being shares on which an aggregate sum has been paid up equal to not less than one-tenth of the total sum paid up on all the shares conferring that right;

    and a demand by a person as proxy for a member shall be the same as a demand by the member.

49. Unless a poll is duly demanded a declaration by the chairman that a resolution has been carried or carried unanimously, or by a particular

Articles of Association (continued)

majority, or lost, or not carried by a particular majority and an entry to that effect in the minutes of the meeting shall be conclusive evidence of the fact without proof of the number or proportion of the votes recorded in favour of or against the resolution.

50. The demand for a poll may, before the poll is taken, be withdrawn but only with the consent of the chairman and a demand so withdrawn shall not be taken to have invalidated the result of a show of hands declared before the demand was made.

51. A poll shall be taken as the chairman directs and he may appoint scrutineers (who need not be members) and fix a time and place for declaring the result of the poll. The result of the poll shall be deemed to be the resolution of the meeting at which the poll was demanded.

52. In the case of an equality of votes, whether on a show of hands or on a poll, the chairman shall not be entitled to a casting vote in addition to any other vote he may have.

53. A poll demanded on the election of a chairman or on a question of adjournment shall be taken forthwith. A poll demanded on any other question shall be taken either forthwith or at such time and place as the chairman directs not being more than thirty days after the poll is demanded. The demand for a poll shall not prevent the continuance of a meeting for the transaction of any business other than the question on which the poll was demanded. If a poll is demanded before the declaration of the result of a show of hands and the demand is duly withdrawn, the meeting shall continue as if the demand had not been made.

54. No notice need be given of a poll not taken forthwith if the time and place at which it is to be taken are announced at the meeting at which it is demanded. In any other case at least seven clear days' notice shall be given specifying the time and place at which the poll is to be taken.

55. A resolution in writing executed by or on behalf of each member who would have been entitled to vote upon it if it had been proposed at a general meeting at which he was present shall be as effectual as if it had been passed at a general meeting duly convened and held and may consist

Articles of Association (continued)

of several instruments in the like form each executed by or on behalf of one or more members.

Votes of members

56. Subject to any rights or restrictions attached to any shares, on a show of hands every member who (being an individual) is present in person or (being a corporation) is present by a duly authorised representative, not being himself a member entitled to vote, shall have one vote and on a poll every member shall have one vote for every share of which he is the holder.

57. In the case of joint holders the vote of the senior who tenders a vote, whether in person or by proxy, shall be accepted to the exclusion of the votes of the other joint holders; and seniority shall be determined by the order in which the names of the holders stand in the register of members.

58. A member in respect of whom an order has been made by any court having jurisdiction (whether in the United Kingdom or elsewhere) in matters concerning mental disorder may vote, whether on a show of hands or on a poll, by his receiver, curator bonis or other person authorised in that behalf appointed by that court, and any such receiver, curator bonis or other person may, on a poll, vote by proxy. Evidence to the satisfaction of the directors of the authority of the person claiming to exercise the right to vote shall be deposited at the office, or at such other place as is specified in accordance with the articles for the deposit of instruments of proxy, not less than 48 hours before the time appointed for holding the meeting or adjourned meeting at which the right to vote is to be exercised and in default the right to vote shall not be exercisable.

59. No member shall vote at any general meeting or at any separate meeting of the holders of any class of shares in the company, either in person or by proxy, in respect of any share held by him unless all moneys presently payable by him in respect of that share have been paid.

60. No objection shall be raised to the qualification of any voter except at the meeting or adjourned meeting at which the vote objected to is tendered, and every vote not disallowed at the meeting shall be valid. Any objection made in due time shall be referred to the chairman whose decision shall be final and conclusive.

Articles of Association (continued)

61. On a poll votes may be given either personally or by proxy. A member holding shares in a public company may appoint more than one proxy to attend on the same occasion, a member of a private company shall only be entitled to appoint one proxy.

62. The appointment of a proxy shall be executed by or on behalf of the appointor and shall be in the following form (or in a form as near thereto as circumstances allow or in any other form which is usual or which the directors may approve) –

     PLC/Limited

     'I/We,   , of   , being a member/members of the above-named company, hereby appoint
                    of   ,
     or failing him,   of   ,
     as my/our proxy to vote in my/our name(s) and on my/our behalf at the annual/extraordinary general meeting of the company to be held on
          year   , and at any adjournment thereof.

     Signed on   year   ?

63. Where it is desired to afford members an opportunity of instructing the proxy how he shall act the appointment of a proxy shall be in the following form (or in a form as near thereto as circumstances allow or in any other form which is usual or which the directors may approve) –

     PLC/Limited

     'I/We,   , of   , being a member/members of the above-named company, hereby appoint
                    of   ,
     or failing him,   of   ,
     as my/our proxy to vote in my/our name(s) and on my/our behalf at the annual/extraordinary general meeting of the company, to be held on
          year   , and at any adjournment thereof. This form is to
be used in respect of the resolutions mentioned below as follows:

     Resolution No. 1   *for *against
     Resolution No. 2   *for *against

     * *Strike out whichever is not desired*

Articles of Association (continued)

Unless otherwise instructed, the proxy may vote as he thinks fit or abstain from voting.

Signed this   day of   year   ?

64. The appointment of a proxy and any authority under which it is executed or a copy of such authority certified notarially or in some other way approved by the directors may –

(a) in the case of an instrument in writing be deposited at the office or at such other place within the United Kingdom as is specified in the notice convening the meeting or in any instrument of proxy sent out by the company in relation to the meeting not less than 48 hours before the time for holding the meeting or adjourned meeting at which the person named in the instrument proposes to vote; or

(b) in the case of an appointment contained in an electronic communication, where an address has been specified for the purpose of receiving electronic communications-

   (i) in the notice convening the meeting, or

   (ii) in any instrument of proxy sent out by the company in relation to the meeting, or

   (iii) in any invitation contained in an electronic communication to appoint a proxy issued by the company in relation to the meeting,

   be received at such address not less than 48 hours before the time for holding the meeting or adjourned meeting at which the person named in the appointment proposes to vote; or

(c) in the case of a poll taken more than 48 hours after it is demanded, be deposited or received as aforesaid after the poll has been demanded and not less than 24 hours before the time appointed for the taking of the poll; or

(d) where the poll is not taken forthwith but is taken not more than 48 hours after it was demanded, be delivered at the meeting at which the poll was demanded to the chairman or to the secretary or to any director; and an instrument of proxy which is not deposited, delivered or received in a manner so permitted shall be invalid.

Articles of Association (continued)

In this article and the next, 'address' in relation to electronic communications, includes any number or address used for the purposes of such communications.

65. A vote given or poll demanded by proxy or by the duly authorised representative of a corporation shall be valid notwithstanding the previous determination of the authority of the person voting or demanding a poll unless notice of the determination was received by the company at the office or at such other place at which the instrument of proxy was duly deposited or, where the appointment of the proxy was contained in an electronic communication, at the address at which such appointment was duly received before the commencement of the meeting or adjourned meeting at which the vote is given or the poll demanded or (in the case of a poll taken otherwise than on the same day as the meeting or adjourned meeting) the time appointed for taking the poll.

Number of directors

66. The maximum and minimum number of directors may be determined by the company by the passing of an ordinary resolution. In the absence of such a resolution there shall be no maximum number of directors and the minimum number of directors shall be one. Whenever there is a sole director that person shall have authority to exercise all the powers and discretions expressed to be vested in the directors generally by these articles.

Alternate directors

67. Any director (other than an alternate director) may appoint any other director, or any other person approved by resolution of the directors and willing to act, to be an alternate director and may remove from office an alternate director so appointed by him.

68. An alternate director shall be entitled to receive notice of all meetings of directors and of all meetings of committees of directors of which his appointor is a member, to attend and vote at any such meeting at which the director appointing him is not personally present, and generally to perform all the functions of his appointor as a director in his absence but shall not be entitled to receive any remuneration from the company for his services as an alternate director. But it shall not be necessary to give

Articles of Association (continued)

notice of such a meeting to an alternate director who is absent from the United Kingdom.

69. An alternate director shall cease to be an alternate director if his appointor ceases to be a director; but, if a director retires by rotation or otherwise but is reappointed or deemed to have been reappointed at the meeting at which he retires, any appointment of an alternate director made by him which was in force immediately prior to his retirement shall continue after his reappointment.

70. Any appointment or removal of an alternate director shall be by notice to the company signed by the director making or revoking the appointment or in any other manner approved by the directors.

71. Save as otherwise provided in the articles, an alternate director shall be deemed for all purposes to be a director and shall alone be responsible for his own acts and defaults and he shall not be deemed to be the agent of the director appointing him.

Powers of directors

72. Subject to the provisions of the Act, the memorandum and the articles and to any directions given by special resolution, the business of the company shall be managed by the directors who may exercise all the powers of the company. No alteration of the memorandum or articles and no such direction shall invalidate any prior act of the directors which would have been valid if that alteration had not been made or that direction had not been given. The powers given by this article shall not be limited by any special power given to the directors by the articles and a meeting of directors at which a quorum is present may exercise all powers exercisable by the directors.

73. The directors may, by power of attorney or otherwise, appoint any person to be the agent of the company for such purposes and on such conditions as they determine, including authority for the agent to delegate all or any of his powers.

Delegation of directors' powers

74. The directors may delegate any of their powers to any committee consisting of one or more directors. They may also delegate to any

Articles of Association (continued)

managing director or any director holding any other executive office such of their powers as they consider desirable to be exercised by him. Any such delegation may be made subject to any conditions the directors may impose, and either collaterally with or to the exclusion of their own powers and may be revoked or altered. Subject to any such conditions, the proceedings of a committee with two or more members shall be governed by the articles regulating the proceedings of directors so far as they are capable of applying.

Appointment of directors

75. The directors shall not be required to retire by rotation.

76. No person shall be appointed a director at any general meeting unless –

(a) he is recommended by the directors; or

(b) not less than fourteen nor more than thirty-five clear days before the date appointed for the meeting, notice executed by a member qualified to vote at the meeting has been given to the company of the intention to propose that person for appointment stating the particulars which would, if he were so appointed, be required to be included in the company's register of directors with notice executed by that person of his willingness to be appointed.

77. Not less than seven nor more than twenty-eight clear days before the date appointed for holding a general meeting notice shall be given to all who are entitled to receive notice of the meeting of any person who is recommended by the directors for appointment as a director at the meeting or in respect of whom notice has been duly given to the company of the intention to propose him at the meeting for appointment as a director. The notice shall give the particulars of the person which would, if he were so appointed, be required to be included in the company's register of directors.

78. Subject as aforesaid, the company may by ordinary resolution appoint a person who is willing to act to be a director either to fill a vacancy or as an additional director.

79. The directors may appoint a person who is willing to act to be a director, either to fill a vacancy or as an additional director, provided that the

Articles of Association (continued)

appointment does not cause the number of directors to exceed any number fixed by or in accordance with the articles as the maximum number of directors.

Disqualification and removal of directors

80. The office of a director shall be vacated if –

(a) he ceases to be a director by virtue of any provision of the Act or he becomes prohibited by law from being a director; or

(b) he becomes bankrupt or makes any arrangement or composition with his creditors generally; or

(c) he is, or may be, suffering from mental disorder and either –

    (i)   he is admitted to hospital in pursuance of an application for admission for treatment under the Mental Health Act 1983 or, in Scotland, an application for admission under the Mental Health (Scotland) Act 1960, or

    (ii)   an order is made by a court having jurisdiction (whether in the United Kingdom or elsewhere) in matters concerning mental disorder for his detention or for the appointment of a receiver, curator bonis or other person to exercise powers with respect to his property or affairs; or

(d) he resigns his office by notice to the company; or

(e) he shall for more than six consecutive months have been absent without permission of the directors from meetings of directors held during that period and the directors resolve that his office be vacated.

Remuneration of directors

81. The directors shall be entitled to such remuneration as the company may by ordinary resolution determine and, unless the resolution provides otherwise, the remuneration shall be deemed to accrue from day to day.

Directors' expenses

82. The directors may be paid all travelling, hotel, and other expenses properly incurred by them in connection with their attendance at meetings of directors or committees of directors or general meetings or separate

Articles of Association (continued)

meetings of the holders of any class of shares or of debentures of the company or otherwise in connection with the discharge of their duties.

Directors' appointments and interests

83. Subject to the provisions of the Act, the directors may appoint one or more of their number to the office of managing director or to any other executive office under the company and may enter into an agreement or arrangement with any director for his employment by the company or for the provision by him of any services outside the scope of the ordinary duties of a director. Any such appointment, agreement or arrangement may be made upon such terms as the directors determine and they may remunerate any such director for his services as they think fit. Any appointment of a director to an executive office shall terminate if he ceases to be a director but without prejudice to any claim to damages for breach of the contract of service between the director and the company. A managing director and a director holding any other executive office shall not be subject to retirement by rotation.

84. Subject to the provisions of the Act, and provided that he has disclosed to the directors the nature and extent of any material interest of his, a director notwithstanding his office –

(a) may be a party to, or otherwise interested in, any transaction or arrangement with the company or in which the company is otherwise interested;

(b) may be a director or other officer of, or employed by, or a party to any transaction or arrangement with, or otherwise interested in, any body corporate promoted by the company or in which the company is otherwise interested; and

(c) shall not, by reason of his office, be accountable to the company for any benefit which he derives from any such office or employment or from any such transaction or arrangement or from any interest in any such body corporate and no such transaction or arrangement shall be liable to be avoided on the ground of any such interest or benefit.

85. For the purposes of article 82 –

(a) a general notice given to the directors that a director is to be regarded

Articles of Association (continued)

as having an interest of the nature and extent specified in the notice in any transaction or arrangement in which a specified person or class of persons is interested shall be deemed to be a disclosure that the director has an interest in any such transaction of the nature and extent so specified; and

(b) an interest of which a director has no knowledge and of which it is unreasonable to expect him to have knowledge shall not be treated as an interest of his.

Directors' gratuities and pensions

86. The directors may provide benefits, whether by the payment of gratuities or pensions or by insurance or otherwise, for any director who has held but no longer holds any executive office or employment with the company or with any body corporate which is or has been a subsidiary of the company or a predecessor in business of the company or of any such subsidiary, and for any member of his family (including a spouse and a former spouse) or any person who is or was dependent on him, and may (as well before as after he ceases to hold such office or employment) contribute to any fund and pay premiums for the purchase or provision of any such benefit.

Proceedings of directors

87. Subject to the provisions of the articles, the directors may regulate their proceedings as they think fit. A director may, and the secretary at the request of a director shall, call a meeting of the directors. It shall not be necessary to give notice of a meeting to a director who is absent from the United Kingdom. Questions arising at a meeting shall be decided by a majority of votes. In the case of an equality of votes, the chairman shall not have a second or casting vote. A director who is also an alternate director shall be entitled in the absence of his appointor to a separate vote on behalf of his appointor in addition to his own vote.

88. The quorum for the transaction of the business of the directors may be fixed by the directors and unless so fixed at any other number shall be two. A person who holds office only as an alternate director shall, if his appointor is not present, be counted in the quorum.

Articles of Association (continued)

89. The continuing directors or a sole continuing director may act notwithstanding any vacancies in their number, but, if the number of directors is less than the number fixed as the quorum, the continuing directors or director may act only for the purpose of filling vacancies or of calling a general meeting.

90. The directors may appoint one of their number to be the chairman of the board of directors and may at any time remove him from that office. Unless he is unwilling to do so, the director so appointed shall preside at every meeting of directors at which he is present. But if there is no director holding that office, or if the director holding it is unwilling to preside or is not present within five minutes after the time appointed for the meeting, the directors present may appoint one of their number to be chairman of the meeting.

91. All acts done by a meeting of directors, or of a committee of directors, or by a person acting as a director shall, notwithstanding that it be afterwards discovered that there was a defect in the appointment of any director or that any of them were disqualified from holding office, or had vacated office, or were not entitled to vote, be as valid as if every such person has been duly appointed and was qualified and had continued to be a director and had been entitled to vote.

92. A resolution in writing signed by all the directors entitled to receive notice of a meeting of directors or of a committee of directors shall be as valid and effectual as if it had been passed at a meeting of directors or (as the case may be) a committee of directors duly convened and held and may consist of several documents in the like form each signed by one or more directors; but a resolution signed by an alternate director need not also be signed by his appointor and, if it is signed by a director who has appointed an alternate director, it need not be signed by the alternate director in that capacity.

93. Provided that his interest has been disclosed a director may vote at any meeting of the directors or a committee thereof on any resolution, notwithstanding that the resolution in any way concerns the director or relates to a matter where the director has a direct or indirect interest, and if the director does vote his vote shall be counted, and in relation to the

Articles of Association (continued)

resolution he shall (whether he has voted or not) be taken into account in calculating the quorum present at the meeting.

94. If a question arises at a meeting of directors or of a committee of directors as to the right of a director to vote, the question may, before the conclusion of the meeting, be referred to the chairman of the meeting and his ruling in relation to any director other than himself shall be final and conclusive.

Secretary

95. Subject to the provisions of the Act, the secretary shall be appointed by the directors for such term, at such remuneration and upon such conditions as they may think fit; and any secretary so appointed may be removed by them.

Minutes

96. The directors shall cause minutes to be made in books kept for the purpose –

    (a) of all appointments of officers made by the directors; and

    (b) of all proceedings at meetings of the company, of the holders of any class of shares in the company, and of the directors, and of committees of directors, including the names of the directors present at each such meeting.

The seal

97. If a company has a seal the seal shall only be used by the authority of the directors or of a committee of directors authorised by the directors. The directors may determine who shall sign any instrument to which the seal is affixed and unless otherwise so determined it shall be signed by a director and by the secretary or by a second director.

Dividends

98. Subject to the provisions of the Act, the company may by ordinary resolution declare dividends in accordance with the respective rights of the members, but no dividend shall exceed the amount recommended by the directors.

Articles of Association (continued)

99. Subject to the provisions of the Act, the directors may pay interim dividends if it appears to them that they are justified by the profits of the company available for distribution. If the share capital is divided into different classes, the directors may pay interim dividends on shares which confer deferred or non-preferred rights with regard to dividend as well as on shares which confer preferential rights with regard to dividend, but no interim dividend shall be paid on shares carrying deferred or non-preferred rights if, at the time of payment, any preferential dividend is in arrear. The directors may also pay at intervals settled by them any dividend payable at a fixed rate if it appears to them that the profits available for distribution justify the payment. Provided the directors act in good faith they shall not incur any liability to the holders of shares conferring preferred rights for any loss they may suffer by the lawful payment of an interim dividend on any shares having deferred on non-preferred rights.

100. Except as otherwise provided by the rights attached to shares, all dividends shall be declared and paid according to the amounts paid up on the shares on which the dividend is paid. All dividends shall be apportioned and paid proportionately to the amounts paid up on the shares during any portion or portions of the period in respect of which the dividend is paid; but, if any share is issued on terms providing that it shall rank for dividend as from a particular date, that share shall rank for dividend accordingly.

101. A general meeting declaring a dividend may, upon the recommendation of the directors, direct that it shall be satisfied wholly or partly by the distribution of assets and, where any difficulty arises in regard to the distribution, the directors may settle the same and in particular may issue fractional certificates and fix the value for distribution of any assets and may determine that cash shall be paid to any member upon the footing of the value so fixed in order to adjust the rights of members and may vest any assets in trustees.

102. Any dividend or other moneys payable in respect of a share may be paid by cheque sent by post to the registered address of the person entitled or, if two or more persons are the holders of the share or are jointly entitled to it by reason of the death or bankruptcy of the holder, to the registered

Articles of Association (continued)

address of that one of those persons who is first named in the register of members or to such person and to such address as the person or persons entitled may in writing direct. Every cheque shall be made payable to the order of the person or persons entitled or to such other person as the person or persons entitled may in writing direct and payment of the cheque shall be a good discharge to the company. Any joint holder or other person jointly entitled to a share as aforesaid may give receipts for any dividend or other moneys payable in respect of the share.

103. No dividend or other moneys payable in respect of a share shall bear interest against the company unless otherwise provided by the rights attached to the share.

104. Any dividend which has remained unclaimed for twelve years from the date when it became due for payment shall, if the directors so resolve, be forfeited and cease to remain owing by the company.

Accounts

105. No member shall (as such) have any right of inspecting any accounting records or other book or document of the company except as conferred by statute or authorised by the directors or by ordinary resolution of the company.

Capitalisation of profits

106. The directors may with the authority of an ordinary resolution of the company –

(a) subject as hereinafter provided, resolve to capitalise any undivided profits of the company not required for paying any preferential dividend (whether or not they are available for distribution) or any sum standing to the credit of the company's share premium account or capital redemption reserve;

(b) appropriate the sum resolved to be capitalised to the members who would have been entitled to it if it were distributed by way of dividend and in the same proportions and apply such sum on their behalf either in or towards paying up the amounts, if any, for the time being unpaid on any shares held by them respectively, or in paying up in full unissued shares or debentures of the company of a nominal amount

Articles of Association (continued)

equal to that sum, and allot the shares or debentures credited as fully paid to those members, or as they may direct, in those proportions, or partly in one way and partly in the other: but the share premium account, the capital redemption reserve, and any profits which are not available for distribution may, for the purposes of this article, only be applied in paying up unissued shares to be allotted to members credited as fully paid;

(c) make such provision by the issue of fractional certificates or by payment in cash or otherwise as they determine in the case of shares or debentures becoming distributable under this article in fractions; and

(d) authorise any person to enter on behalf of all the members concerned into an agreement with the company providing for the allotment to them respectively, credited as fully paid, of any shares or debentures to which they are entitled upon such capitalisation, any agreement made under such authority being binding on all such members.

Notices

107. Any notice to be given to or by any person pursuant to the articles (other than a notice calling a meeting of the directors) shall be in writing or shall be given using electronic communications to an address for the time being notified for that purpose to the person giving the notice. In this article, 'address', in relation to electronic communications, includes any number or address used for the purposes of such communication.

108. The company may give any notice to a member either personally or by sending it by post in a prepaid envelope addressed to the member at his registered address or by leaving it at that address or by giving it using electronic communications to an address for the time being notified to the company by the member. In the case of joint holders of a share, all notices shall be given to the joint holder whose name stands first in the register of members in respect of the joint holding and notice so given shall be sufficient notice to all the joint holders. A member whose registered address is not within the United Kingdom and who gives to the company an address within the United Kingdom at which notices may be given to him, or an address to which notices may be sent using electronic

Articles of Association (continued)

communications, shall be entitled to have notices given to him at that address, but otherwise no such member shall be entitled to receive any notice from the company. In this article and the next, 'address', in relation to electronic communications, includes any number or address for the purposes of such communications.

109. A member present, either in person or by proxy, at any meeting of the company or of the holders of any class of shares in the company shall be deemed to have received notice of the meeting and, where requisite, of the purposes for which it was called.

110. Every person who becomes entitled to a share shall be bound by any notice in respect of that share which, before his name is entered in the register of members, has been duly given to a person from whom he derives his title.

111. Proof that an envelope containing a notice was properly addressed, prepaid and posted shall be conclusive evidence that the notice was given. Proof that a notice contained in an electronic communication was sent in accordance with guidance issued by the Institute of Chartered Secretaries and Administrators shall be conclusive evidence that the notice was given. A notice shall, unless the contrary is proved, be deemed to be given at the expiration of 48 hours after the envelope containing it was posted or, in the case of a notice contained in an electronic communication, at the expiration of 48 hours after the time it was sent.

112. A notice may be given by the company to the persons entitled to a share in consequence of the death or bankruptcy of a member by sending or delivering it, in any manner authorised by the articles for the giving of notice to a member, addressed to them by name, or by the title of representatives of the deceased, or trustee of the bankrupt or by any like description at the address, if any, within the United Kingdom supplied for that purpose by the persons claiming to be so entitled. Until such an address has been supplied, a notice may be given in any manner in which it might have been given if the death or bankruptcy had not occurred.

Winding up

113. If the company is wound up, the liquidator may, with the sanction of an

Articles of Association (continued)

extraordinary resolution of the company and any other sanction required by the Act, divide among the members in specie the whole or any part of the assets of the company and may, for that purpose, value any assets and determine how the division shall be carried out as between the members or different classes of members. The liquidator may, with the like sanction, vest the whole or any part of the assets in trustees upon such trusts for the benefit of the members as he with the like sanction determines, but no member shall be compelled to accept any assets upon which there is a liability.

Special provision

114. In the event of the company having no members and no directors as the result of the death or deaths of the members and/or directors the personal representative of the last member to die has the right by notice in writing to appoint a director of the company and this appointment shall have the same effect as if made in a general meeting. Where due to circumstances resulting in the death of two or more members or directors it is uncertain which of them survived the longest it shall be assumed that death occurred in the order of seniority, thus the younger will be assumed to have outlived the elder.

Indemnity

115. Subject to the provisions of the Act but without prejudice to any indemnity to which a director may otherwise be entitled, every director or other officer or auditor of the company shall be indemnified out of the assets of the company against any liability incurred by him in defending any proceedings, whether civil or criminal, in which judgment is given in his favour or in which he is acquitted or in connection with any application in which relief is granted to him by the court from liability for negligence, default, breach of duty or breach of trust in relation to the affairs of the company.

Articles of Association (continued)

Signature(s), name(s) and address(es) of subscriber(s):

1.   Signature   _____

       Name   _____

       Address   _____

                     _____

2.   Signature   _____

       Name   _____

       Address   _____

                     _____

Dated this _____ day of _____ year _____

Witness to the above signature

Signature   _____

Name   _____

Address   _____

                  _____

Share Certificate

Certificate No. _____

Number of Shares _____

This is to Certify that _____

of _____

is/are the Registered holder(s) of _____ shares of £ _____ each _____ paid

in the above-named Company, subject to the Memorandum and Articles of Association of the Company.

*This document is hereby executed by the Company /

The Common Seal of the Company was hereto affixed in the presence of:

_____ Directors

_____ Secretary

_____ 20 ___

* *Delete as appropriate*

Example Share Certificates

Certificate No. ___1___   Number of Shares ___1___

Lawpack Publishing Limited

This is to Certify that Alexander Palmer

of 85 Preston Square, London SW6 5CN

is/are the Registered holder(s) of ___1___ shares of £ ___1___ each ___fully___ paid
in the above-named Company, subject to the Memorandum and Articles of Association of the Company.

*This document is hereby executed by the Company /
~~The Common Seal of the Company was hereto affixed in the presence of:~~

Julia Etheridge
Julia Etheridge   Directors
A Palmer
Alexander Palmer   Secretary   11th January ___ 20 05

* Delete as appropriate

Certificate No. ___2___   Number of Shares ___1___

Lawpack Publishing Limited

This is to Certify that Julia Etheridge

of 16 St. George's Crescent, Reading RG7 9XY

is/are the Registered holder(s) of ___1___ shares of £ ___1___ each ___fully___ paid
in the above-named Company, subject to the Memorandum and Articles of Association of the Company.

*This document is hereby executed by the Company /
~~The Common Seal of the Company was hereto affixed in the presence of:~~

Julia Etheridge
Julia Etheridge   Directors
A Palmer
Alexander Palmer   Secretary   11th January ___ 20 05

* Delete as appropriate

Example Form 10: First directors and secretary and intended situation of registered office

10

Please complete in typescript, or in bold black capitals.
CHWP000
Notes on completion appear on final page

First directors and secretary and intended situation of registered office

Company Name in full

Lawpack Publishing Limited

Proposed Registered Office
(PO Box numbers only, are not acceptable)

1 James Road

Post town

County / Region | London | Postcode | EC1 7OP

If the memorandum is delivered by an agent for the subscriber(s) of the memorandum mark the box opposite and give the agent's name and address.

Agent's Name | N/A

Address

Post town

County / Region | | Postcode

Number of continuation sheets attached

You do not have to give any contact information in the box opposite but if you do, it will help Companies House to contact you if there is a query on the form. The contact information that you give will be visible to searchers of the public record.

Alexander Palmer

Lawpack Publishing Limited, 1 James Road

London EC1 7OP   Tel   020 7123 4567

DX number   DX exchange

Companies House receipt date barcode
This form has been provided free of charge by Companies House

v 08/02

When you have completed and signed the form please send it to the Registrar of Companies at:
Companies House, Crown Way, Cardiff, CF14 3UZ   DX 33050 Cardiff
for companies registered in England and Wales
or
Companies House, 37 Castle Terrace, Edinburgh, EH1 2EB
for companies registered in Scotland   DX 235 Edinburgh
                                                    or LP - 4 Edinburgh 2

Example Form 10: First directors and secretary and intended situation of registered office (continued)

Company Secretary (see notes 1-5)

Company name	Lawpack Publishing Limited	

NAME *Style / Title: Mr   *Honours etc:

* Voluntary details

Forename(s): Alexander

Surname: Palmer

Previous forename(s):

Previous surname(s):

†† Tick this box if the address shown is a service address for the beneficiary of a Confidentiality Order granted under section 723B of the Companies Act 1985 otherwise, give your usual residential address. In the case of a corporation or Scottish firm, give the registered or principal office address.

Address †† : 85 Preston Square

London

Post town:

County / Region: Postcode: SW6 5CN

Country:

I consent to act as secretary of the company named on page 1

Consent signature *A Palmer*   **Date** 03-01-05

Directors (see notes 1-5)

Please list directors in alphabetical order

NAME *Style / Title: Mr   *Honours etc:

Forename(s): Alexander

Surname: Palmer

Previous forename(s):

Previous surname(s):

†† Tick this box if the address shown is a service address for the beneficiary of a Confidentiality Order granted under section 723B of the Companies Act 1985 otherwise, give your usual residential address. In the case of a corporation or Scottish firm, give the registered or principal office address.

Address †† : 85 Preston Square

London

Post town:

County / Region: Postcode: SW6 5CN

Country:

Date of birth: Day 0 3 Month 0 2 Year 1 9 5 5   **Nationality** British

Business occupation: Company Director

Other directorships: None

I consent to act as director of the company named on page 1

Consent signature *A Palmer*   **Date** 03-01-05

Example Form 10: First directors and secretary and intended situation of registered office (continued)

Directors (see notes 1-5)
Please list directors in alphabetical order

NAME *Style / Title	Ms	*Honours etc
*Voluntary details	**Forename(s)** Julia	
	Surname Etheridge	
	Previous forename(s)	
	Previous surname(s)	

†† Tick this box if the address shown is a service address for the beneficiary of a Confidentiality Order granted under section 723B of the Companies Act 1985 otherwise, give your usual residential address. In the case of a corporation or Scottish firm, give the registered or principal office address.

Address ††

	16 St. George's Crescent
	Reading
Post town	
County / Region	Postcode RG7 9XY
Country	

Date of birth

Day	Month	Year					
2	9	0	9	1	9	5	7

Nationality British

Business occupation Sales Executive

Other directorships Additional Co. Ltd.

I consent to act as director of the company named on page 1

Consent signature *Julia Etheridge* **Date** 03-01-05

This section must be signed by either an agent on behalf of all subscribers or the subscribers (i.e those who signed as members on the memorandum of association).	**Signed** *A Palmer*	**Date** 03-01-05
	Signed *Julia Etheridge*	**Date** 03-01-05
	Signed	**Date**
	Signed	**Date**
	Signed	**Date**
	Signed	**Date**
	Signed	**Date**

Example Form 10: First directors and secretary and intended situation of registered office (continued)

Notes

1. Show for an individual the full forename(s) NOT INITIALS and surname together with any previous forename(s) or surname(s).

   If the director or secretary is a corporation or Scottish firm - show the corporate or firm name on the surname line.

   Give previous forename(s) or surname(s) except that:

   - for a married woman, the name by which she was known before marriage need not be given,

   - names not used since the age of 18 or for at least 20 years need not be given.

   A peer, or an individual known by a title, may state the title instead of or in addition to the forename(s) and surname and need not give the name by which that person was known before he or she adopted the title or succeeded to it.

   Address:

   Give the usual residential address.

   In the case of a corporation or Scottish firm give the registered or principal office.

   Subscribers:

   The form must be signed personally either by the subscriber(s) or by a person or persons authorised to sign on behalf of the subscriber(s).

2. Directors known by another description:

   - A director includes any person who occupies that position even if called by a different name, for example, governor, member of council.

3. Directors details:

   - Show for each individual director the director's date of birth, business occupation and nationality. **The date of birth must be given for every individual director.**

4. Other directorships:

   - Give the name of every company of which the person concerned is a director or has been a director at any time in the past 5 years. You may exclude a company which either **is** or at **all times during the past 5 years,** when the person was a director, **was**:

   - dormant,

   - a parent company which wholly owned the company making the return,

   - a wholly owned subsidiary of the company making the return, or

   - another wholly owned subsidiary of the same parent company.

   If there is insufficient space on the form for other directorships you may use a separate sheet of paper, which should include the company's number and the full name of the director.

5. Use Form 10 continuation sheets or photocopies of page 2 to provide details of joint secretaries or additional directors.

Example Form 12: Declaration on application for registration

12

Declaration on application for registration

Please complete in typescript, or in bold black capitals.

CHWP000

Company Name in full | Lawpack Publishing Limited

I, | Alexander Palmer

of | 85 Preston Square, London SW6 5CN

† Please delete as appropriate.

do solemnly and sincerely declare that I am a † [Solicitor engaged in the formation of the company][person named as director or secretary of the company in the statement delivered to the Registrar under section 10 of the Companies Act 1985] and that all the requirements of the Companies Act 1985 in respect of the registration of the above company and of matters precedent and incidental to it have been complied with.

And I make this solemn Declaration conscientiously believing the same to be true and by virtue of the Statutory Declarations Act 1835.

Declarant's signature | *A Palmer*

Declared at | 4 Richton Way, Exeter EX1 2DN

| Day | Month | Year |

On | 0 3 | 0 1 | 2 0 0 5

❶ Please print name.

before me ❶ | Campbell Bush

Signed | *Campbell Bush* | **Date** | 03-01-05

† A Commissioner for Oaths or Notary Public or Justice of the Peace or Solicitor

You do not have to give any contact information in the box opposite but if you do, it will help Companies House to contact you if there is a query on the form. The contact information that you give will be visible to searchers of the public record.

Alexander Palmer

Lawpack Publishing Limited, 1 James Road

London EC1 7OP | Tel 020 7123 4567

DX number | DX exchange

Companies House receipt date barcode

This form has been provided free of charge by Companies House.

Form revised 10/03

When you have completed and signed the form please send it to the Registrar of Companies at:
Companies House, Crown Way, Cardiff, CF14 3UZ DX 33050 Cardiff
for companies registered in England and Wales
or
Companies House, 37 Castle Terrace, Edinburgh, EH1 2EB
for companies registered in Scotland DX 235 Edinburgh
or LP - 4 Edinburgh 2

Example Form G88(2): Return of allotment of shares

Please complete in typescript, or in bold black capitals.
CHWP000

88(2)
Return of Allotment of Shares

Company Number | 1234567

Company name in full | Lawpack Publishing Limited

Shares allotted (including bonus shares):

	From			To		
Date or period during which shares were allotted *(If shares were allotted on one date enter that date in the "from" box)*	Day	Month	Year	Day	Month	Year
	1 1	0 1	2 0 0 5			

Class of shares *(ordinary or preference etc)*	Ordinary		
Number allotted	2		
Nominal value of each share	1		
Amount (if any) paid or due on each share *(including any share premium)*	1		

List the names and addresses of the allottees and the number of shares allotted to each overleaf

If the allotted shares are fully or partly paid up otherwise than in cash please state:

% that each share is to be treated as paid up	N/A		

Consideration for which the shares were allotted *(This information must be supported by the duly stamped contract or by the duly stamped particulars on Form 88(3) if the contract is not in writing)*	N/A

Companies House receipt date barcode

When you have completed and signed the form send it to the Registrar of Companies at:

Companies House, Crown Way, Cardiff CF14 3UZ   DX 33050 Cardiff
For companies registered in England and Wales

Companies House, 37 Castle Terrace, Edinburgh EH1 2EB
For companies registered in Scotland   DX 235 Edinburgh
or LP - 4 Edinburgh 2

Example Form G88(2): Return of allotment of shares (continued)

Names and addresses of the allottees *(List joint share allotments consecutively)*

Shareholder details		Shares and share class allotted	
		Class of shares allotted	Number allotted
Name: Alexander Palmer			
Address: 85 Preston Square		Ordinary	1
London			
UK Postcode S W 6 5 C N			
Name: Julia Etheridge			
Address: 16 St. George's Crescent		Ordinary	1
Reading			
UK Postcode R G 7 9 X Y			
Name:			
Address:			
UK Postcode			
Name:			
Address:			
UK Postcode			
Name:			
Address:			
UK Postcode			

Please enter the number of continuation sheets (if any) attached to this form

Signed *A Palmer*   Date 06-02-05

A director / secretary / administrator / administrative receiver / receiver manager / receiver   *Please delete as appropriate*

You do not have to give any contact information in the box opposite but if you do, it will help Companies House to contact you if there is a query on the form. The contact information that you give will be visible to searchers of the public record.

Tel

DX number   DX exchange

Example Form 123: Notice of increase in nominal capital

COMPANIES FORM No. 123

G

**Notice of increase
in nominal capital**

123

CHWP000

Please do not
write in
this margin

Pursuant to section 123 of the Companies Act 1985

*Please complete
legibly, preferably
in black type, or
bold block lettering*

To the Registrar of Companies
(Address overleaf)

For official use

Company number

1234567

Name of company

* insert full name
of company

★ Lawpack Publishing Limited

gives notice in accordance with section 123 of the above Act that by resolution of the company

dated _____11th January 2005_____ the nominal capital of the company has been

increased by £ ___900_____ beyond the registered capital of £ ___100_____ .

† the copy must be
printed or in some
other form approved
by the registrar

A copy of the resolution authorising the increase is attached. †

The conditions (eg. voting rights, dividend rights, winding-up rights etc.) subject to which the new

shares have been or are to be issued are as follows :

Please see Articles of Association of the company.

Please tick here if
continued overleaf

‡ Insert
Director,
Secretary,
Administrator,
Administrative
Receiver or
Receiver
(Scotland) as
appropriate

Signed *A Palmer*   Designation ‡ Director   Date 11-01-05

Presentor's name address and
reference (if any) :

Alexander Palmer
Lawpack Publishing Limited
1 James Road
London EC1 7OP

For official Use
General Section

Post room

Example Form 225: Change of accounting reference date

225

Please complete in typescript,
or in bold black capitals

CHWP000

Change of accounting reference date

Company Number 1234567

Company Name in Full Lawpack Publishing Limited

NOTES
You may use this form to change the accounting date relating to either the current or the immediately previous accounting period.

a. You **may not** change a period for which the accounts are already overdue.

b. You **may not** extend a period beyond 18 months unless the company is subject to an administration order.

c. You **may not** extend periods more than once in five years unless:

1. the company is subject to an administration order, or

2. you have the specific approval of the Secretary of State, (please enclose a copy), or

3. you are extending the company's accounting reference period to align with that of a parent or subsidiary undertaking established in the European Economic Area, or

4. the form is being submitted by an oversea company.

The accounting reference period ending

Day	Month	Year
3 1	0 1	2 0 0 7

is **shortened** ✓ so as to end on
extended ☐

please tick appropriate box

Day	Month	Year
3 1	1 2	2 0 0 6

Subsequent periods will end on the same day and month in future years.

If extending more than once in five years, please indicate in the box the number of the provision listed in note c. on which you are relying.

Signed *A Palmer* **Date** 11th January 2005

† Please delete as appropriate

† a director / secretary / administrator / administrative receiver / receiver and manager / receiver (Scotland) / person authorised on behalf of an oversea company

You do not have to give any contact information in the box opposite but if you do, it will help Companies House to contact you if there is a query on the form. The contact information that you give will be visible to searchers of the public record.

Lawpack Publishing Limited

1 James Road

London EC1 7OP Tel 020 7123 4567

DX number DX exchange

Companies House receipt date barcode

When you have completed and signed the form please send it to the Registrar of Companies at:
Companies House, Crown Way, Cardiff, CF14 3UZ DX 33050 Cardiff
for companies registered in England and Wales **or**
Companies House, 37 Castle Terrace, Edinburgh, EH1 2EB DX 235 Edinburgh
for companies registered in Scotland **or LP - 4 Edinburgh 2**

10/03

Example Format of Minutes of the First Meeting of the Directors

Lawpack Publishing LIMITED

Minutes of the First Meeting of the Directors
held at 1 James Road, London EC1
on 11th January 2005 at 11 a.m.

PRESENT: Alexander Palmer (In the Chair)
Julia Etheridge

1. The Chairman announced that a quorum was present and declared the Meeting open.

2. There were produced to the Meeting the following:

2.1 the Certificate of Incorporation of the Company (under No. 1234567) dated 9th January 2005;

2.2 a copy of the Memorandum and Articles of Association of the Company as registered;

2.3 a copy of Form 10, the statement required under section 10(2) Companies Act 1985 signed by the subscribers to the Memorandum of Association containing:

(i) particulars of the first Directors of the Company and the first Secretary of the Company and their respective consents to act in the relevant capacity; and

(ii) particulars of the intended situation of the registered office of the Company.

3. **IT WAS RESOLVED** that:

3.1 Alexander Palmer and Julia Etheridge each having subscribed to the Memorandum and Articles of Association for one ordinary share of £1 each, one such share be allotted and issued to each of them and certificates be issued in respect of such shares;

3.2 Mr Palmer be and he is hereby appointed Chairman of the Directors;

Example Format of Minutes of the First Meeting of the Directors (continued)

3.3 the register of Directors' interests in shares or debentures of the Company be kept at the registered office of the Company;

3.4 a bank account for the Company be opened with National Bank plc, in accordance with the mandate lodged with the Bank;

3.5 Messrs. Maxwells of 10 North Court, Manchester, Chartered Accountants, be and they are hereby appointed Auditors of the Company and their remuneration shall be agreed by the Board;

3.6 the second accounting reference period of the Company be changed so as to be from 31st January 2006 to 31st December 2006 and consequently 31st December shall be the date on which in each successive calendar year an accounting reference period of the Company is to be treated as coming to an end;

3.7 the Secretary be instructed to arrange for the filing with the Registrar of Companies all necessary returns, including:

(i) Form G88(2) (Return of allotment of shares);

(ii) Form 225 (Change of accounting reference date).

There being no further business the Meeting was closed.

A. Palmer

Chairman

Example Format of Written Resolution of All the Directors

Lawpack Publishing LIMITED

Resolution of all the Directors in Office

Pursuant to Article 92 of the Company's Articles of Association dated 3rd January 2005

The Directors hereby confirm that they have before them the following:

1. The Certificate of Incorporation of the Company (under No. 1234567) dated 9th January 2005.

2. A copy of the Memorandum and Articles of Association of the Company as registered.

3. A copy of Form 10, the statement required under section 10(2) Companies Act 1985 signed by the subscribers to the Memorandum of Association containing:

    (i) Particulars of the first Directors of the Company and the first Secretary of the Company and their respective consent to act in the relevant capacity;

    (ii) Particulars of the intended situation of the registered office of the Company.

IT WAS RESOLVED that:

1. Alexander Palmer and Julia Etheridge having subscribed to the Memorandum and Articles of Association for one ordinary share of £1 each, one share be allotted and issued to each of them and certificates be issued in respect of such shares.

2. The register of the Director's interests in shares or debentures of the Company be kept at the registered office of the Company.

3. A bank account for the Company be opened with National Bank plc in accordance with the mandate lodged with the bank.

4. Messrs. Maxwells of 10 North Court, Manchester, Chartered Accountants

Example Format of Written Resolution of All the Directors (continued)

be and they are hereby appointed Auditors of the Company and their remuneration shall be agreed by us as Directors.

5. The second accounting reference period of the Company be changed so as to be from the 31st January 2006 to 31st December 2006 and consequently 31st December shall be the date on which in each successive calendar year an accounting reference period of the Company is to be treated as coming to an end.

6. The Secretary be instructed to arrange for the filing with the Registrar of Companies of all necessary returns including:

   (i) Form G88(2) (Return of allotment of shares);

   (ii) Form 225 (Change of accounting reference date).

A. Palmer

Director

Julia Etheridge

Director

Examples of Registers

Register of Members

Name	Alexander Palmer
Address	85 Preston Square, London SW6 5CN

Date of entry as shareholder __04-01-05__ Date of cessation of membership _____

Date of Allotment OR Entry of Transfer	References in Register		Number of shares	No.of Share Certificate	Amount paid or agreed to be considered as paid	Acquisitions
	Allotments	Transfers				
11-01-05	✓		1	1	£1	

Dividends to ____ Alexander Palmer ____

Class of Share ____ Ordinary ____ Denomination ____ £1 each ____

Disposals	Balance	£	emarks
	£1		

Name	Julia Etheridge
Address	16 St. George's Crescent, Reading RG7 9XY

Date of entry as shareholder _____ Date of cessation of membership _____

Date of Allotment OR Entry of Transfer	References in Register		Number of shares	No.of Share Certificate	Amount paid or agreed to be considered as paid	Acquisitions
	Allotments	Transfers				
11-01-05	✓		1	2	£1	

Dividends to ____ Julia Etheridge ____

Class of Share ____ Ordinary ____ Denomination ____ £1 each ____

Disposals	Balance	£	emarks
	£1		

Register of Directors

Surname (or Corporate Name) __Palmer__

Forenames(s) __Alexander__

any former Forenames or Surnames _____

Nationality __British__ Date of Birth __03-02-55__

Residential Address (or Registered or Principal Office __85 Preston Square, London SW6 5CN__

	Date of Resignation
Other Directorships ____ None ____	

Business Occupation ____ Company Director ____

Date of Appointment __03-01-05__ minute __11-01-05__

Date of filing particulars __03-01-05__

Date of Resignation or Cessation _____ minute _____

Date of filing particulars _____

Surname (or Corporate Name) __Etheridge__

Forenames(s) __Julia__

any former Forenames or Surnames _____

Nationality __British__ Date of Birth __29-09-57__

Residential Address (or Registered or Principal Office __16 St. George's Crescent, Reading RG7 9XY__

	Date of Resignation
Other Directorships __Additional Co. Ltd.__	

Business Occupation ____ Sales Executive ____

Date of Appointment __03-01-05__ minute __11-01-05__

Date of filing particulars __03-01-05__

Date of Resignation or Cessation _____ minute _____

Date of filing particulars _____

Surname (or Corporate Name) _____

Forenames(s) _____

any former Forenames or Surnames _____

Nationality _____ Date of Birth _____

Residential Address (or Registered or Principal Office _____

	Date of Resignation
Other Directorships _____	

Business Occupation _____

Date of Appointment _____ minute_____

Date of filing particulars _____

Date of Resignation or Cessation _____ minute _____

Date of filing particulars _____

0405269

Examples of Registers (continued)

Register of Secretaries

Surname (or Corporate Name) _Palmer_	Residential Address (or Registered or Principal Office) _85 Preston Square, London SW6 5CN_
Forenames(s) _Alexander_	
any former Forenames or Surnames	
Date of Appointment _03-01-05_ minute _11-01-05_	Date of Resignation or Cessation _____ minute_____
Date of filing particulars	Date of filing particulars
Surname (or Corporate Name)	Residential Address (or Registered or Principal Office)
Forenames(s)	
any former Forenames or Surnames	
Date of Appointment _____ minute _____	Date of Resignation or Cessation _____ minute_____
Date of filing particulars	Date of filing particulars
Surname (or Corporate Name)	Residential Address (or Registered or Principal Office)
Forenames(s)	
any former Forenames or Surnames	
Date of Appointment _____ minute _____	Date of Resignation or Cessation _____ minute_____
Date of filing particulars	Date of filing particulars
Surname (or Corporate Name)	Residential Address (or Registered or Principal Office)
Forenames(s)	
any former Forenames or Surnames	
Date of Appointment _____ minute _____	Date of Resignation or Cessation _____ minute_____
Date of filing particulars	Date of filing particulars
Surname (or Corporate Name)	Residential Address (or Registered or Principal Office)
Forenames(s)	
any former Forenames or Surnames	
Date of Appointment _____ minute _____	Date of Resignation or Cessation _____ minute_____
Date of filing particulars	Date of filing particulars

Register of Directors' Interests

Name and Address of Person Interested _Alexander Palmer_
85 Preston Square, London SW6 5CN

Classes of Share Capital or Debentures _Ordinary shares_
(a) 1 share of £1 each
(b)

Entry	Date of			Nature of Event	No. of shares involved		No. of Shares in which interested after event	Price consideration	Remarks
No.	Date	Event	Notification		Acquisitions	Disposals			
1	4-1-05	3-1-05	4-1-05	Subscriber to Memorandum of Association	1		1	£1	

Name and Address of Person Interested _Julia Etheridge_
16 St. George's Crescent, Reading RG7 9XY

Classes of Share Capital or Debentures _Ordinary shares_
(a) 1 share of £1 each
(b)

Entry	Date of			Nature of Event	No. of shares involved		No. of Shares in which interested after event	Price consideration	Remarks
No.	Date	Event	Notification		Acquisitions	Disposals			
2	4-1-05	3-1-05	4-1-05	Subscriber to Memorandum of Association	1		1	£1	

0405269

Example Format of Notice of Extraordinary General Meeting

LAWPACK PUBLISHING LIMITED
(Registered in England No. 1234567)

Notice of Extraordinary General Meeting

NOTICE IS HEREBY GIVEN that an Extraordinary General Meeting of the above-named Company will be held at 1 James Road, London EC1 on 25th of January 2005 at 2:00 p.m. for the purpose of considering and, if thought fit, passing the following resolutions of which the resolution numbered 1 will be proposed as an ordinary resolution and the resolution numbered 2 will be proposed as a special resolution:

Ordinary Resolution

1. That the authorised share capital of the Company be and is hereby increased from £100 to £1,000 by the creation of 900 Ordinary Shares of £1 each.

Special Resolution

2. That the name of the Company be changed to 'Lawpack Software Limited'.

By Order of the Board

A. Palmer
Secretary

Dated 19th January 2005

Registered Office: 1 James Road London EC1 7OP

Note:

A member entitled to attend and vote at the Extraordinary General Meeting convened by this notice may appoint a proxy to attend and (on a poll) vote in his stead. A proxy need not be a member of the Company.

An instrument appointing a proxy should be completed and deposited at the registered office of the Company not less than 48 hours before the time of the Meeting specified above or of the adjourned meeting at which the proxy proposes to vote.

Example Format of Consent to Short Notice of Extraordinary General Meeting

LAWPACK PUBLISHING LIMITED

Form of Consent to Short Notice
of
Extraordinary General Meeting

We, the undersigned, being a majority in number of the Members of the Company having the right to attend and vote at the Extraordinary General Meeting of the Company to be held 25th January 2005 ('the Meeting') and together holding not less than 95 per cent in nominal value of the shares giving that right, hereby agree that the Meeting shall be deemed to have been duly convened and held and that the resolutions set out in the notice of the Meeting may be proposed and passed as ordinary and special resolutions notwithstanding that less than the requisite notice thereof as specified in the Companies Act 1985 or in the Company's Articles of Association has been given.

A Palmer

Alexander Palmer

Julia Etheridge

Julia Etheridge

Dated: 19th January 2005

Example Format of Minutes of Extraordinary General Meeting

LAWPACK PUBLISHING LIMITED

**Minutes of an Extraordinary General Meeting of the Company
held at 1 James Road, London EC1
on 25th January 2005 at 2.00 p.m.**

PRESENT: Alexander Palmer (In the Chair)
              Julia Etheridge

1. The Chairman announced that the meeting had been properly convened and constituted and that as a quorum was present, declared the Meeting open.

2. The Chairman announced that the necessary majority of the members of the Company had consented to the holding of the Meeting at short notice.

3. The Chairman proposed that the authorised share capital of the Company be and is hereby increased from £100 to £1,000 by creating 900 ordinary shares of £1 each and such ordinary resolution was passed unanimously.

4. The Chairman proposed that the name of the company be changed to 'Lawpack Software Limited' and such special resolution was passed unanimously.

5. There being no further business, the Chairman declared the Meeting closed.

A. Palmer
Chairman

Example Format of Ordinary and Special Resolutions

Company No. 1234567

COMPANIES ACT 1985
COMPANY LIMITED BY SHARES

**Ordinary and Special Resolutions of
Lawpack Publishing Limited**

(Passed 25th January 2005)

At an Extraordinary General Meeting of the above-named company duly convened and held on 25th January 2005 the following resolutions were duly passed as ordinary and special resolutions respectively:

Ordinary Resolution

1.   That the authorised share capital of the Company be and is hereby increased from £100 to £1,000 by the creation of 900 ordinary shares of £1 each.

Special Resolution

2.   That the name of the company be changed to 'Lawpack Software Limited'.

A. Palmer
_____
Chairman

Example Format of Elective Resolutions Passed as Written Shareholders' Resolutions

Company No. 1234567

LAWPACK PUBLISHING LIMITED

Written Shareholders' Resolutions

PURSUANT TO the Articles of Association of the Company we, the undersigned being all the members of the Company entitled to attend and vote at General Meetings of the Company HEREBY AGREE AND CONFIRM that the following resolutions shall be as valid and effectual as if they had been passed as elective resolutions at a General Meeting of the Company duly convened and held accordingly we HEREBY RESOLVE:

1. THAT in accordance with the provisions of Section 252 of the Companies Act 1985 the Company hereby dispenses with the laying of accounts and reports before the Company in General Meeting in respect of the year ending 31st January 2005 and subsequent financial years.

2. THAT in accordance with the provision of Section 366A of the Companies Act 1985 the Company hereby dispenses with the holding of the Annual General Meeting for 2005 and subsequent years.

3. THAT in accordance with the provisions of Section 386 of the Companies Act 1985 the Company hereby dispenses with the obligation to appoint auditors annually and that during the term that the dispensation is in force the directors be and they are hereby authorised to fix the auditors' remuneration.

A Palmer

Alexander Palmer

Julia Etheridge

Julia Etheridge

Dated: 11th January 2005

Note:
The above wording is sufficient if the company is relying on the written resolution

Example Format of Elective Resolutions Passed as Written Shareholders' Resolutions (continued)

procedures contained within the Articles of Association. However if the company has auditors and/or is relying on the written resolution procedures contained in the Companies Act 1985, the above preamble should read:

'Pursuant to the provisions of Section 381A of the Companies Act 1985 we, the undersigned being all the members of the Company entitled to attend and vote at General Meetings of the Company HEREBY AGREE AND CONFIRM that the following resolutions shall be as valid and effectual as if they had been passed as elective resolutions at a General Meeting of the Company duly convened and held accordingly we HEREBY RESOLVE:'

Index

This index covers main text and endmatter. An 'e' after a page number indicates an example document and/or example text; a 'g' indicates a glossary entry.

A
accountants 70e
accounting reference dates 23-4, 46, 47g, 104e
accounting reference periods 23-4, 47g
accounts 27, 28-9, 46, 47g, 89e, 104e
 bank accounts 23
 exemptions 24-5
 scope 23-4
 share premium accounts 36
allotment of shares 22, 45, 47g, 66-7e, 101-2e
Annual General Meetings (AGMs) *see* shareholders' meetings
Annual Return (Form 363) 27-8
Articles of Association 17-18, 37, 46, 47g, 63-93e
assets 47g
 dividends from 88e
 shares from 25
audited accounts *see* accounts
auditors 23, 28
 replacement of 44

auditor's reports 28, 29
authorised capital 47g

B
bank accounts 23
bankruptcy
 liquidation 33, 91-2e
 notice from 91e
 share transmission from 71-2e
Board 47g *see also* directors
Board meetings 21, 47g
 accounts from 23-5
 asset transferral from 25
 chairperson 86e, 113e
 exemptions 32-3
 notice 32
 quorums 32, 85-6e
 recording 27, 32, 87e, 105-6e, 113e
 share certificates from 22-3
 share issues from 22
 taxation from 25-6
 voting 32, 85e, 86-7e
 see also shareholders' meetings

C
calls on shares 66-7e
capital 4
  authorised capital 47g
  share capital 5, 9, 35, 36, 45,
    64e, 72e, 103e
capitalisation of profits 89-90e
casting votes 32, 39, 76e
Certificate of Incorporation 19
chairperson 32, 39, 74-5e, 76e,
  86e, 113e
Change of Accounting Reference
  Date (Form 225) 24, 104e
clear days' notice 38, 47g, 73e
companies 1-2, 4, 5-6 *see also*
  individual terms
Companies Act 1985 22 *see also*
  individual documents
Companies House viii, 15, 19, 22,
  27-8, 29, 41, 43, 45 *see also*
    individual documents
continuity 5
costs 5
criminal offences 33
  in use of names 55-8
'Cyfyngedig' in registered names
  11, 12, 15

D
death
  director appointments after 92e
  notice from 91e
  share transmission from 71-2e
debts, transferral 25
Declaration on Application for
  Registration (Form 12) 18, 100e
directors 9, 17, 18, 27-8, 35, 45,
  47g
  alternate 80-1e
  appointment of 33, 82-3e, 84e,
    92e

chairperson 32, 39, 74-5e, 76e,
  86e, 113e
contributions from 33
delegation from 81-2e
expenses 83-4e
gratuities 85e
interests 84-5e, 86-7e
meetings *see* Board meetings
numbers 80e
payment 83e
pensions 85e
powers 31, 81e, 86e
replacement of 31-2, 83e
responsibilities 32
scope 33
see also individual documents
directors' reports 28, 29
dividends 87-9e
documents *see individual*
  documents
'dormant' companies 25

E
EGMs *see* shareholders' meetings
elective resolutions 29, 48g, 115-16e
electronic communication 10
  for notice 90-1e
  for proxy appointments 79e, 80e
  for returns 28
employment, taxation 25
expenses 83-4e
Extraordinary General Meetings
  see shareholders' meetings

F
fees 10
financial years 23-4
fines 28
First Directors and Secretary
  and...Registered Office (Form
    10) 16-17, 96-9e

Form 10 16-17, 96-9e
Form 12 18, 100e
Form 123 103e
Form 225 24, 104e
Form 363 27-8
Form G88(2) 22, 101-2e
fraudulent trading 33

G
general meetings *see* shareholders'
    meetings
gratuities 85e
guarantees 6

H
HM Revenue & Customs 25-6

I
incorporation 48g
    amendments after *see* post-
        incorporation amendments
    electronic 10
    fees 10
    minimum criteria 9-10
    paper-based 10 *see also*
        individual documents
    practice from *see individual*
        terms
indemnity 92e
issue of shares 22, 35-6, 48g

L
liability
    limited 2, 4, 6, 7
    unlimited 3, 6
lien for shares 65-6e
limited companies 1-2, 4, 5-6 *see*
    also individual terms
'Limited' in registered names 11,
    12, 15
limited liability 2, 4, 6, 7

liquidation 33, 91-2e

M
meetings *see* Board meetings;
    shareholders' meetings
members 48g, 109e *see also*
    shareholders; subscribers
Memorandum of Association 16,
    22, 48g, 61-2e
    objects clause 45
mental health
    on directorships 83e
    on voting 77e
minute book 27, 32, 87e
minutes 27, 32, 48g, 87e, 105-6e,
    113e

N
names *see* registered names
notice 32, 75e, 111-12e
    on auditors 44
    clear days' 38, 47g, 73e
    for director appointments 82e
    for poll voting 76e
    for proxies 79e, 80e
    scope 38, 73-4e, 90-1e
    for share capital 103e
    short 38
    special notice 31
    for transferral 68-70e
Notice of Increase in Nominal
    Capital (Form 123) 103e

O
objects clause 45
office, registered 13, 26, 44, 48g,
    96e
online communication 10
    for notice 90-1e
    for proxy appointments 79e,
        80e

for returns 28
online forms *see individual documents*
ordinary resolutions 40, 41, 44, 45, 114e

P

partnership businesses 3-4
payment 83e
    of dividends 87-9e
    for shares 36, 65e, 66-7e
pensions 85e
poll votes 40, 48g
    notice 76e
    proxies 77e, 78-9e, 80e
    scope 75-6e, 77e
post-incorporation amendments 10, 29
    on accounting reference dates 23-4, 46, 47g, 104e
    on Articles of Association 46
    on auditors 44
    on Memorandum of Association 45
    on registered names 45
    on registered office 44
    scope 43, 44
    on secretary 43
    on share allotment 45
    on share capital 45, 103e
pre-emption 48g
premises, registered names in 12
prices of shares 70e
private limited companies 1-2, 4, 5-6 *see also individual terms*
profits, capitalisation of 89-90e
proxies 39, 48g
    appointment of 79e, 80e
    for voting 77e, 78-9e, 80e
public limited companies 7

Q

quorums 32, 39, 48g, 74e, 85-6e

R

record keeping 26-7 *see also individual documents*; accounts; minutes
Register of Directors 109e
Register of Directors' Interests 110e
Register of Members 22, 109e
Register of Secretaries 110e
registered names 45
    'Cyfyngedig' in 11, 12, 15
    exemptions 11
    'Limited' in 11, 12, 15
    in premises 12
    restrictions 11, 51-8
    on stationery 12, 13
    trade marks and 12
    trade names and 13
registered office 13, 26, 44, 48g, 96e
registers 26
    Register of Directors 109e
    Register of Directors' Interests 110e
    Register of Members 22, 109e
    Register of Secretaries 110e
registration 12, 13, 100e *see also individual terms*
resolutions
    elective resolutions 29, 48g, 115-16e
    ordinary resolutions 40, 41, 44, 45, 114e
    scope 49g
    special resolutions 40-1, 45, 114e
    written *see* written resolutions

Return of Allotment of Shares (Form G88(2)) 22, 101-2e
returns
  electronic 28
  fines 28
  paper-based 27-8

S

seal 23, 27, 87e
secretary 9, 17, 27-8, 33-4, 43, 87e
  see also individual documents
share capital 5, 9, 35, 36, 45, 64e, 72e
  notice 103e
share certificates 22-3, 49g, 64-5e, 94-5e
share premium accounts 36
shareholders 18, 35, 36, 49g, 115- 16e
  liability 2, 4, 6, 7
  powers 31-2
  proxies for 39
  scope 37
  see also individual documents; members; subscribers
shareholders' meetings 36, 37, 48g
  adjournments 75e
  chairperson 74-5e
  for director appointments 82e
  exemptions 29, 41
  notice 31, 38, 73-4e, 75e, 111-12e
  proxies 39
  quorums 39, 74e
  recording 27, 113e
  scope 73e
  voting 39-40, 75-80e
  see also Board meetings
shares 2, 4, 6, 7, 16
  allotment 22, 45, 47g, 66-7e, 101-2e

from assets 25
calls 66-7e
capital from 5, 9, 35, 36, 45, 64e, 72e, 103e
certificates for 22-3, 49g, 64-5e, 94-5e
dividends 87-9e
forfeiture 67-8e
issue 22, 35-6, 48g
lien 65-6e
payment 36, 65e, 66-7e
pre-emption 48g
prices 70e
purchase by company 73e
transferral 18, 37, 68-71e
transmission 71-2e
show of hands votes 39, 76e, 77e
single-member companies 22, 74e
'small' companies 24-5
sole trader businesses 2-3
special notice 31
special resolutions 40-1, 45, 114e
stationery, registration details on 12, 13
statutory books 26, 49g
subscribers 16, 18, 22, 49g *see also individual documents*; members; shareholders

T

taxation 3, 25-6
trade marks, registered names and 12
trade names, registered names and 13
transfer notices 68e

U

unlimited liability 3, 6

V

Value Added Tax (VAT) 25-6
voting 86-7e
   casting votes 32, 39, 76e
   for ordinary resolutions 40, 41
   poll votes 40, 48g, 75-6e, 77e,
      78-80e
   scope 76-7e, 85e
   show of hands votes 39, 76e,
      77e
   for special resolutions 40-1

W

Welsh language 11, 12, 15, 28
winding up 91-2e
written resolutions 21, 32, 41,
      76-7e, 86e, 107-8e, 115-16e
   accounts from 23-5
   share certificates from 22-3
   share issues from 22
wrongful trading 33